The Woodstove Widow

Sara Sousa

2020
Durham, NC

ISBN: 9798634995397

Dedicated to:

David, June, Debbie, and Zach

Author's Note

The light gray boxes titled, "**In Greg's Words**," throughout this book contain writing taken directly from Greg's journal. Nothing was changed or edited.

Table of Contents

Prologue, July 2010

It started with a fly, buzzing between our living room windows. One fly became two, barely noticed as out of the ordinary in the Carolina summer heat. Two flies became four, then twelve. We yelled at the kids for lingering with the back door open when headed out to play. Twelve flies became thirty. Our home was an entomologic horror movie. It wasn't the kids.

A bit of sleuthing led us to the fireplace, ground zero of our fly epidemic. We opened the glass panels to find dozens of fat, swarming flies. Greg called a local chimney sweep. They found and removed a dead squirrel, cleaned the chimney, and put a cap on the top to prevent further rodents from falling to their death. In talking with the service person, Greg learned about a woodstove insert – a wood burning stove that fits into the fireplace, generating warmth and a pretty view from the couch on a cold night.

We decided to install an insert, a touch of Little House on the Prairie in our suburban, North Carolina home. Our first winter, we turned to Craigslist postings and roadway signs next to woodpiles to stock our firewood. After one season of spending too much money on too little firewood, Greg began gathering his own BTUs. He bought a cheap, used trailer. He bought an expensive maul from the Swedish company, Gränsfors Bruk. He bought beeswax wood polish and conditioner for the maul's handle. He networked with other wood burners. He learned the frustrations of trying to split sinewy, tough sweet gum and of trying to differentiate fallen gum from oak, with no tell-tale leaves or gumballs left behind. He learned how to swing a maul with impressive accuracy and strength. He learned when to keep swinging and when to step away, tossing the knotted mass aside.

Greg loved splitting wood. It was physical, therapeutic, and productive. We delighted in our perfectly toasty house – a warm, cozy living room and cooler upstairs bedrooms. The kids would come downstairs in the morning and eat cereal in front of the dancing, orange flames. I put a strip of masking tape down the middle of the half-circle, wool rug in front of the stove, to assuage the incessant bickering over who was hogging the coveted real estate. The woodstacks found their rhythm – growing with the appearance of fireflies, shrinking after the first frost. Much to Greg's delight, our heat pump almost never came on in the winter – sitting silent for weeks as the ash pile grew in the back. The woodstove became part of our daily winter life.

The Seizure, June 2012

In Greg's Words

Summary of Events

Nothing prior to Jun 21, no signals, nothing. Of note, I pedaled from home to New Hope Overlook on Jordan Lake on Jun 17, 25 beautiful miles, departing home around 5:20a. The bike ride was during the dawn of the day, few cars, amazing world. At New Hope Overlook I entered an organized event, a one mile swim. Think about odds and the lottery ticket, what if my grand mal hit on Jun 17 at the approximate 0.5 mile turn buoy?

Jun 21, grand mal seizure in Montgomery, AL during a work trip. I estimate it happened around 15:15 local time. Seizure at client's office. 911 call and EMT ride to hospital in Montgomery. Chest x-ray at ER was clean. CT scan in AL showed calcification and mass in right front brain. EKG was clean. Begin Depakote. The client stayed by my side, on Jun 20 he left the office to go propose to his fiancée, on Jun 21 he returned to his office to capitalize on training from me. He got about 45 minutes of me and then I was done. He was the primary witness and he accompanied me to the ER. He described me as arching back and out of my chair, making incoherent guttural utterances, and convulsing for 1 – 2 minutes. After the convulsing, it was a period of observed haze and fogginess. Eventually, my perception of haze and fogginess started to occur, that was coincident to the arrival of the EMT. I estimate that across the next 45 – 60 minutes I was able to get my senses back. When it was time to talk to my wife, that was the time I started crying. Very frustrating that when I get her, I can't communicate, I pass the phone to my advocate and he connects with her.

Jun 22, I returned to the client's office to pick up the laptop and notebook, but the first thing I notice is the streaks I left on his office wall, it was my blood. I quickly went to the bathroom to get some damped paper towels and returned to clean my blood off his wall. My friend drove from Atlanta to Montgomery to get me on Jun 21, on Jun 22 he drove me back to Atlanta. Sara drove to Atlanta and met me there. We slept in Atlanta.

Jun 23, Sara and I drove back to Durham.

Jun 25, two appts in Durham, one PCP and one neurosurgeon. Neurosurgeon says mass is too big and my brain is squished. He said it is likely not a rapid, malignant tumor.

Jun 26, MRI with contrast at Duke.

Jun 28, neurosurgeon says it is likely tumor, hopefully benign. He asks me what I want to do.

Jul 03, face-to-face appt with neurosurgeon to discuss plan. I have a 2-inch diameter tumor on my right front brain. It shows some hints of tentacle outreach at this time. He recommends removing it in a timely manner. Open skull, pull out material. Doc said he does not issue high confidence on what the tumor is until he gets patho report. His angle so far is not rapid malignant. I go in on Jul 10 and sleep at Duke Hosp. Surgery on Jul 11. I sleep in ICU on Jul 11. I sleep outside of ICU but still at Duke on Jul 12. My first sleep night at home is Friday the Thirteenth. Setting up 6 week leave from work. First 1-2 weeks should be dynamic recovery period. Then weeks 3 through 6 are slower recovery. Anti-seizure medicine for 1 year. No car for 6 months. Pathology report at 3 days after surgery is the magic key, its results have significant meaning on what future prognosis is, things such as whether I do or do not get fixed schedule MRIs, etc.

Currently, no drive car, no bike, no breaking in chainsaw. Though is a nice period of zero alcohol and so far zero soda.

I am planning to skate through this without a loss of function, but I understand the possible outcomes. I give them respect of acknowledgement and no more, we need to focus on the healthy outcomes. It is scary, better to mess with my hand, or foot, not my brain. The experience of seizure, I was blacked out. It is the come-out of seizure that I remember, and that is one heck of an experience I hope to never repeat.

I will never forget Greg's phone call from the emergency department in Alabama, the feelings are still visceral. There was a strange, crackly message on the answering machine. I caught that Greg was in the ED and they were running some tests. He left a phone number – either a co-worker's number or the number of a nurse in the ED. I went out to our back porch to call back, away from the children. I could tell that something was very wrong. He'd had a seizure and a CT revealed a brain lesion. At the time, I didn't even consider cancer. I decided that "lesion" was a generic term that could mean almost anything. In my imagination, I pictured a small wisp of something, perhaps a bit of scar tissue left from a childhood concussion. I got off the phone and called my parents, my body pulsing with anxiety and adrenaline. I was overcome with sobbing as I explained Greg's call. Over the next few hours, we sorted out the details of my getting to Greg and of having Belle and Abe cared for. I remember nothing else from this day.

The First Surgery, July 2012

In Greg's Words

GDS Ramblings

Lots to think of, focusing on the "skate through" side, but aware of other. Tier 1 stays to get through this healthy and with no loss of cognitive function. Lower goal is to still get me to Shut-In* this year, hopefully my slowest, hopefully to complete. Anyway, many many sub-stories happen from observing complex life through too many faces in hallways, dropoff/pickup, elevator, and waiting rooms; the various manifestations of ill health in this life. I reflect lots upon the many vibrant things I have been granted to do to this point so far. I bask in the comfort that I made many good choices when I could have chosen other. I well up thinking about the family Sara has raised, and the family I came from. I pay attention to the dynamics revealed between Sara and I as we sit through the various discussions with many people about sawing into my skull, uncertainty of offshoots from the mass in my brain, what (if any) brain damage I have, and if I will come out of this calling every person I meet "Shirley". I have many goals and ambitions I still hunger deeply to achieve, but they begin with being there for my family. Jingle jangle go the nerves, each sweetness and pain goes this life.

Evening Before Surgery:
On steroids now, with a hyper active side effect. Bad for sleeping. But I am in the chemical world now, so Depakote to take me down, steroids which result in stimulating, and then a sleeping pill to make me downer. All ages on my oncology floor. I had another MRI tonight with markers, I saw others down at MRI that did look messed up. Is tough, as expected. I await now for bosswoman to make her arrival. But she gets the laz-E-boy chair, tough for me in chivalry to accept.

I try to keep laugh going as a way to prepare. I thought of telling Belle that the reason they are working on my head is because I am pregnant. And when a man is pregnant the baby is in his head. Since I have no vagina in my head they have to cut my skull to get the baby out. However, I have not thought through how to explain to her when I am after surgery and I have no baby, thus I may not try that strategy of explanation on her…yet.

Out of ICU, in Regular Room:
At hospital for hopefully last night. I run the range. Slight blood goop droops down the side of my head. Many medications. I do need to be careful of being silly PARTICULARLY in neuro ward, where how you speak is used to assess condition. I likely still have a rough path. But there are also discussions of a functional path.

**Shut-In is an annual, 18-mile trail run in Asheville, NC.*

I've put off writing, feeling like I should write something positive about how amazing Greg is and about his fantastic medical team and about how strong he is. I know this to be true, but I'm just not there right now. Finding out that your life partner has a brain mass sucks as much as you imagine it sucks. Meeting with the neurosurgeon after surgery is as nerve wracking as you imagine it is. Seeing your husband sunk down in an ICU bed looking like he was hit head-on by a truck is as miserable as you'd imagine. I spent a good part of the day reading stories from the

"Living with Cancer" magazine in the OR waiting room – stories full of cancer patients navigating their disease with positive attributes like humor and grace. Our story is still unfolding, but for right now, phew, it's tough.

Post-op

I have come back from the Dark Side (10 minutes with Greg will do that to a person). He is oh-so-much better today than last evening. He still looks beat up, but his spirit is fully intact – beat up and upbeat, go figure. Once again, all who care for him come into his room with straight, set lips and walk out with a smile (and a few more jokes in their back pocket). When I'm by his side, he'll throw out a classic – "Have you met my wife?" he asks. The person shakes their head no. "This is my wife, Sara. She is a six-figure woman. [pause for effect] She's got five in her salary [makes an hourglass shape with his fingers] and ooh, la, la, this is her sixth." The combination of Greg's sincerity and the look on my face usually elicits either a guffaw or an amused eye roll and head shake. Greg should be discharged home tomorrow. Everyone's love and energy reached its destination and we are buoyed up and looking ahead.

Back Home

Greg made it home after an uneventful discharge. It helps that I'm a nurse, able to understand dressing change orders, new medications, and signs and symptoms that warrant an outreach to the on-call team. We're fairly smitten with Greg's neuro-oncology providers. Many of the clinicians we met at the hospital, will continue to follow Greg from here on out. We hope that the pathology results reveal that we won't need to spend much time with them. Greg came home, ate a bunch of veggies and hummus, and went upstairs to sleep. All is calm, for now.

Day One at home involved lots of sleep for Greg. Wake up, eat breakfast, sleep, eat lunch, sleep, putter around the house and yard, sleep, eat dinner, spend time with family, sleep. He is up and about, able to converse and laugh, sits down to family meals, and is generally pleasant. All of these things are truly miraculous given what he's been through this week. Neighbors and friends proclaim, "Wow, you look really good!" Even so, I have to stop myself from saying aloud "Seriously????"

If you ran into Greg after not seeing him for a couple of months and had no idea of what has been going on, you might say something like "Holy [insert preferred explicative], what happened to you?" His usual athletic gait is slow and his posture hunched, the top of his head is a puffy and swollen, he has two black eyes, there is dried blood in his ears, and he has an extremely impressive head wound. His incision runs from ear to ear across the top of his head along his hair line. The neat row of staples makes it look like a creepy zipper. However, if you've been in the loop and know his story, his physical traits are all still intact. His black, curly hair is there, just past the incision. His brown eyes show he's alert and engaged, crinkling at the corners when he smiles. People seem to have imagined brain surgery recovery as having more swelling, more bruising, more blood, and much more laying around incapacitated. If you didn't have your glasses on, or saw him from far away, you wouldn't notice a thing wrong.

I miss the old Greg. I miss his unbruised, unswollen, confident self. I'm still getting used to this "new and improved" Greg – the Survivor of Brain Surgery Extraordinaire. In my mind, I see him running, biking, swimming, throwing the kids in the pool, chopping wood. I know that sooner than we can imagine, he will be back to all of this. The swelling and bruises will be gone, the staples removed, and the energy restored.

In Greg's Words

Pathology

Pathology came back: anaplastic oligodendroglioma. Slow malignant. But good prognosis. More markers were ordered but will not be available by the 2012-07-19 appointment. Still, the 2012-07-19 appointment will be the first pass at making my plan. Reasonable that chemo/radio is in my path, bummer, maybe not.

Ambition 1 stays as recover, be here, be functional. Useful and relevant intermediates such as Shut-In, Swim Around Key West, Bridger Ridge Run sure do hold allure, but cannot rise at this time. Instead smaller events will have to do and being healthy along-the-way.

Sara is the boss. Grateful to all.

"BE STILL!"

People connect with cancer in different ways. Some "fight" cancer, going bravely into battle, armed with chemo, radiation, and indomitable spirits. Others "beat" cancer, standing next to it at the start line and sprinting full force to the finish line. Or, maybe they stand face to face with cancer in the boxing ring, punching hard until there's a knockout. I appreciate humor – I had to chuckle when I first saw a "Save the tatas," pink ribbon bumper sticker. A dear friend whose father recently died from cancer said that when she went bowling the other day, she bowled a strike when she imagined the pins as Greg's tumor – Ka-POW – Gottcha!!!

Am I capable of loving cancer? Can I give it a big hug and whisper gently "settle down little cells, don't be so rambunctious." What would those cells do if I could bathe them in a warm, loving light? Would they settle down? Would they quit being so angry and dividing into space where they don't belong? I'm too much of a pacifist to feel connected to "fighting" cancer. I'm not ready to start loving it either.

The image that clicks for me comes from Maurice Sendak's *Where the Wild Things Are* (Harper & Row,1963). After arriving at the island where the wild things live and witnessing their rowdy and rambunctious behavior, Brave Max commands "BE STILL!" and tames the beasts. I see Greg as Max – mischievous, adventurous, loving, loved. The tumor surely is a wild thing – misbehaving and scary (and, yet, doing the only thing it knows how to do). With beautiful authority, Max commands the wild things to "BE STILL," and they dutifully obey. For now, on our cancer journey, this is the image I'm going with.

"But the wild things cried, "Oh please don't go – we'll eat you up – we love you so!" And Max said, "No!"""

Neuro-oncology Appointment

The doctors won't decide on a final treatment plan until additional pathology results are in. We did get a sense of options at Greg's first follow-up appointment. There will most likely be 12 months of oral chemotherapy. We are waiting to learn about radiation.

We are entering a new world. Those who have been on a cancer journey know this world. The volume and variety of medical appointments is overwhelming – meetings with neurosurgeons, neurooncolgists, neurologists, primary care providers, child life specialists, social workers, phlebotomists, nurses, nurse practitioners, and radiologists. The alternative is unappealing. If we chose not to enter into this new world, then the tumor grows and spreads, replacing normal brain function with unwanted gremlins. Our goal is to move into and through treatment and into a world where Greg is healthy and strong.

A couple of recent, non-brain tumor highlights:

- Last night, Abe slept for the first time with no diaper. He and his bed were dry in the morning.
- Belle shot a bow and arrow yesterday and was very, very excited.
- During a run this morning, I saved a small box turtle from plummeting off a cement bridge onto a pile of rocks.

Staples Gone (almost)

Our day began with Greg getting his staples removed. Almost all came out except for 15 - 20 where additional healing is needed. There is a pocket of fluid along the incision and under his skin, which his body needs to reabsorb. Greg was a bit bummed to not get all of them out. His mental energy is buoyed by completing small, tangible milestones.

Belle came with us this morning. She met the child life specialist, a social worker who works with families on how to talk to children about cancer. We met with her before Greg's surgery and were impressed with her straightforward way of talking about cancer. If the kids seem like they're having a hard time understanding Greg's illness, then she helps us say and do the right things to calm their fears. I thought that Belle would be fascinated with her Daddy getting the staples out, but after watching the nurse studiously pull the thin, metal strips until releasing from his tender skin, all Belle could muster was "ooooh, gross."

Tumor Genetics (and good news)

Greg does not need to start with radiation. His tumor has a genetic type that responds well to chemotherapy alone. Since radiation and brains tend to not go well together, it is good that he does not need radiation. We will get a more specific treatment plan in early August, but we can expect a year of oral chemo with regular MRIs.

My sense of relief surprised me. Clinically, folks who have anaplastic oligodendroglioma with the genetic trait like Greg's tumor do notably better than folks with this type of tumor without this genetic trait.

Below, is a summary of the news we've gotten over the past month, and my internal response:

Greg had a seizure –
Fuck, Greg had a seizure, that's NOT good.

Greg has a lesion on his brain –
Lesion, what the heck is a lesion? Maybe it's nothing.

Greg needs an MRI –
Hmmmm. OK, MRI, we can handle that.

Greg's lesion could be a mass or a tumor –
Shit, mass or tumor, that's NOT good.

Mass or tumor shows characteristics of being benign –
Oh, benign, that's good. Still why is it there?

Greg will need craniotomy to extract tumor –
Fuck, a craniotomy, that's NOT good.

Tumor is oligodendroglioma, maybe grade II, maybe grade III –
Please grade II, oh please grade II.

Tumor is anaplastic oligodendroglioma, grade III –
Fuck, grade III, that's NOT good.

Tumor may have genetic markers that make it a less aggressive variant –
Please less aggressive, oh please less aggressive.

Tumor has less aggressive trait –
Halleluiah!! Halleluiah!!

Now, we focus on rest and recovery until we learn more details about the chemo in August.

Being Prepared

The week of July 4th, two weeks after Greg's seizure in Alabama, we were scheduled for our annual vacation to visit Greg's parents and other family and friends in Rhode Island. We changed our trip such that Belle and Abe flew up stay with their grandparents for the week and Greg and I stayed in Durham to meet with the neurosurgeon and prepare for tumor extraction. It was an odd week. Without two rambunctious little ones to feed and clothe and bathe and play with, we could sleep late, eat quiet meals together, and have a real conversation (even more than one!). We were enveloped by a new sense of anxiety and a frenzy to get "a bunch of stuff" done. We spent much of the week washing and changing dirty bedsheets, sorting through stacks of mail and medical paperwork, and throwing out half-empty containers of condiments and salad dressing with past-due expiration dates.

During this week, I read an article called "Being Prepared" about people called "preppers." (Emily Matchar, Outside Magazine, August 2012). Preppers spend extensive (perhaps excessive) amounts of time and money preparing for an assortment of doomsday scenarios – everything from natural disasters to political collapse to solar flares. They organize their lives such that if some calamity were to befall society as we know it, they would be prepared. Renewable and/or non-perishable food source – check. Potable water supply – check. Non-grid-dependent energy source – check. Medicinal supplies – check. Firewood powered automobile – check. Weapons to keep out the frantic unprepared – check.

There is something appealing, even calming, about preparing for the end of the world. With countless movies and TV shows about various end-of-the-world predictions, our culture has infiltrated our psyche with fear of the unknown. Even respectable and tame outlets like NPR and cable news shows regularly highlight the lurking dangers of political unrest, hurricanes, global warming, and infectious disease outbreaks. While reading the article in Outside, I found myself wanting to run out to REI to at least get a water filter and a book about edible plants of the southeastern United States.

Preppers guess how their life might end and then do something to prevent that outcome. The purpose is to survive the unraveling of society. In this light, their actions really don't make much sense.

I once had a boss nicknamed "Mad Dog" who would say, "Somethin's gonna gettcha" in response to spoken worries about threats to our mortal flesh, like the dangers of smoking or sunbathing. I took her comment to mean that there's no sense in worrying about your death because it's going to happen at some point anyways. She's right. Something is going to get each of us. Our cells eventually run out of steam for one reason or another. Ideally, we've got 80-plus good years under our belt before this happens.

We know a lot about how to stay alive and healthy to age 80 and beyond. We have volumes of data about millions of real people (alive and deceased) which clearly show what we should worry the most about when it comes to our mortality. In the US, it's not hurricanes, political unrest, or infrastructure collapse (and we have seen each of these events on our shores in the past few years, so we're not immune). For those of you who are wondering, the top three are heart disease, cancer, and lung disease. Other big ones in the top ten are accidents, diabetes, and influenza/pneumonia.

There are known measures to prevent (or at least postpone) many of these ailments. The biggest is to not smoke. The list from there goes on – eat a plant-based diet, exercise with some regularity, wear a seatbelt, wear a bike helmet, don't talk on a cell phone while driving, avoid a sunburn, wash hands with warm water and soap while singing "twinkle, twinkle little star", avoid exposure to toxic chemicals, and build a strong social network. I'm curious how many preppers smoke cigarettes, bike without a helmet, or are overweight. Perhaps they've mastered all of the health-promoting lifestyle choices that we know prolong longevity, and have moved onto bigger, less mundane conquests. I doubt it. Their actions suggest that they're hoping to somehow control things that cannot be controlled (like exploding calderas) and they do not trust things that can be controlled (like political processes and infrastructure). I'm not sure that I want to be a part of this world view.

Nothing can explain Greg's brain tumor and there's nothing we could have done differently to prepare for it. And yet, here it is. The dirty little secret is that while there is a lot that we can do to postpone our demise, there is very little we can do to prevent or even prepare for whatever it is that's "gonna gettcha."

The world view of preppers is based on fear and anxiety. The following quote is highlighted in the Outside article, " 'We're living in a time of instability,' Hunt says … 'it doesn't take long for people to turn into animals.' " The preppers sound nervous, fearful, cocky, and lonely. This strikes me as an intense contrast to what we are experiencing because of Greg's cancer. Yes, we are pretty much freaking out, a simmering panic has settled into our core. But more than that, there is this connectedness and compassion and hope.

Greg's tumor is not a death sentence. However, it is a whisper in our ear of that possibility. It is asserting itself as a reminder that we are mortal beings. I can't imagine a prepper starting a blog stating "Hey, I'm really worried that a solar flare is going to wipe out all electronic communications and I won't be able to purchase gas. Then, I won't be able to get to the store to buy food. Please sign up to bring me dinners while I develop a back-up plan."

There's something to be said for living in the here and now, even when the here and now is unsettling and scary. Here we are with a cancer diagnosis. Here we are immersed in a refrigerator full of meals and an entire loving community to walk this road with us. Here we are surrounded by a medical team dedicated to making those cancer cells be still. Here we are learning what it means to be a human in pain who can count on gentle and loving friends to lean on. No guns or water filters or books on edible plants needed, just us.

75

That's the total number of staples removed from Greg's head. The final removal went well (at least from my perspective). The nurse was very gentle with some crusty areas and Greg is now staple free.

On Sunday, Greg ventured back to church – it felt good to be there as a 4-pack again, lined up together in the wooden pew, the simple, black cross anchored before us, red hymnals tucked neatly along the back of the pew in front of us. After church, we had lunch outside with neighbors. Greg is tired. He's in a tricky place, where he is relatively pain free and is getting his energy back, but there is still healing going on beneath his rockin' scar.

So Long July

Even though we don't know what lies ahead, I'm not sad to say, "So long!" to July 2012. I'm getting back into work, although I'm also easily distracted. Part of the distraction is from all that has happened these past few weeks, but I also blame the good-old-fashioned summertime blues. I'd rather be hiking in the mountains or lounging at the beach.

Greg stayed home with the kids today while I went to work. From what I can tell, the only real drama was when some combination of Abe and/ or Belle put stickers on parts of Abe where the sun don't shine (the stories varied as to who did what). Greg undid the damage and instructed them about the importance of avoiding the combination of adhesive with some of the body's more delicate tissues. Based on Belle's feedback, the lesson sunk in (but only time will tell...).

Greg is getting out and about and learning to work around his driving and biking restrictions (he can do neither, right now). He is borrowing a friend's push scooter and using it for small errands. Today, he used the scooter to get to the bus station – he reminded me of a child, heading off on a scooter with his backpack and helmet, one foot resting on the flat, metal surface while the other pushed the two little wheels down the bumpy street. This bit of activity and independence made him happy.

We were supposed to fly out to Montana tomorrow but are postponing our trip until Greg is more recovered. I'm sad not to see my Dad (Grandpa John) and stepmom (Grandma Ramona, or Gramona) and their beautiful ranch. I've visited their ranch since I was a little girl and have many good memories of grasshoppers leaping through the tall grass, mountains still topped with snow in August, and the earthy smell of hay. My MT folks had been refurbishing a cabin on their property for us to stay in for this trip (I think that our rowdy 4-pack, with wacky sleep habits and messy eating, may have been a bit much for their super-nice house). Hopefully soon.

Moving Forward

Today, Greg talked about being between two storms – the first storm was surgery and the next storm is chemo. We're hoping to find little ways to enjoy this relative calm. We're also hoping that chemo won't be too bumpy.

Tonight, we found a stash of small fireworks that had been lying dormant, tucked away on a back shelf in the closet. We invited neighbor kids over to light them. The pyrotechnics were tame, but it was still fun. The kids liked the poppers the best – the little pods that you throw on the ground and they make a satisfying "pop."

Greg e-mailed his neurosurgeon about acceptable post-surgery activity levels. Frustratingly for his engineering brain, there are no hard and fast rules about what he can and can't do. The surgeon's general recommendation is for Greg to self-regulate based on pain and fatigue and also to use common sense. Before surgery, risk of another seizure was a concern. There are many activities that are generally safe, but if a seizure is thrown into the mix, they become catastrophic. Think swimming, driving, biking, operating a chain saw, or even taking a bath.

Now that the tumor is out and Greg is on anti-seizure medicine, the risk of seizure is technically still present, but greatly reduced. The MD gave Greg clearance to do some light biking, after making sure that he did not experience problems with balance (which was a concern that we'd not considered before).

Last night, the four of us took our bikes up to the school behind our house. We pedaled laps on a dirt path that winds around a playground and soccer field. Greg felt fine pedaling around the bumpy path. Belle won the cute award. Her bike is slightly too big for her, but still ridable. She also chose to bring a big backpack with a purple stuffed dog poking out. She went 'round and 'round the path with awesome determination – little girl on big bike, taking on the world.

And, to leave you with a chuckle, Greg's e-mail exchange with the neurosurgeon included the MD stating that he didn't see any reason why Greg would need to use a chainsaw right now. Little does he know ...

We're Just Running in Circles

Tonight, Greg and I joined our local running club for their summer track series at UNC. About 30 people ages 3 to 73 gather at the track, summer heat holding heavy as the sun starts its descent below the surrounding brick buildings. Greg got the OK to do easy runs, so we did a 1500m jog, 100m "dash", 1500m walk, and 400m run. Greg said he felt his legs the most – no concerns regarding his head or balance. Nobody made a big deal about Greg's presence, which was exactly what he needed.

The evening sky was a sunset with layers upon layers of heavy clouds next to thin wispy clouds. There were deep oranges and pinks and dusk purples coming through the breaks.

Tomorrow, Greg has a 7:30a MRI and then a 12:30p meeting with the oncologists. We'll learn more about the chemo plan. I want to see the MRI because I'm curious how it looks with a big chunk of brain missing.

Treatment Plan

We made it through a marathon day at the cancer center. Greg begins chemotherapy on Monday with an oral agent called Temodar, aka temozolomide. The schedule is 5 days on and 23 days off for 12 cycles. The most common side effects are nausea, slowed digestion, and fatigue. Different practitioners told us different things regarding hair loss, so we'll see on that one. Greg will take an anti-nausea pill one hour before the chemo pill. The drug also affects blood counts, so he'll get blood work done on days 21 and 28 of each cycle. During this year of treatment, he'll get an MRI every 2 months. After the 12 cycles of chemotherapy, he'll get a PET scan using radioactive glucose to look for any "hot" cells that may be remaining. The goal is for the PET scan to come back "cold."

Greg started the day with his MRI at 7:30a. Lamar, the MRI technician, helped with at least one of Greg's MRIs at the hospital. He remembered Greg and how much he had staff laughing and smiling. On his way out of the MRI room, with Greg carefully tucked in the tube, Lamar said something like "This guy's great, he's gonna do all right."

After the MRI, we went to Elmos Diner for a late breakfast and then to the Duke Al Buehler trail and walked one circuit. We walked the loop in 51 minutes, escaping the cool, medical environment of the cancer center into the comfort of a dirt path lined with trees and brush, branches arching over the path to give shade from the dense, summer heat. We returned for Greg's oncology appointment and first met with the physician's assistant (PA), who went over some of the basics of chemo. It was a rough meeting, partly because of the content and partly because the PA spoke poor English. Communication was bad enough that Greg didn't make any jokes.

We then met with Greg's neurooncologist, who speaks well and has good bedside manner. She reviewed that morning's MRI. The space where the tumor was fills with blood first and then transitions to cerebral spinal fluid. The brain tissue doesn't grow back, but it does shift to fill in the cavity. The MRI shows that most of the tumor was removed except for a penny sized mass. This mass does not show up as active on the scan, which suggests that it does not contain any fast-growing cells. The goal of the chemo is to shut down any remaining cancer cells.

Finally, we met with the lead oncology RN who went over the nuts and bolts of taking the chemo and scheduling the blood work and appointments. After a bit of a misunderstanding about how we would actually acquire the temozolomide, we went downstairs for Greg to get bloodwork and then to the cancer center pharmacy. We have to wait for insurance to process the paperwork and anticipate picking up the pills later today or Monday.

The day was draining – we were given so much information to process. We try to sift through the hard truth of Greg's cancer to find areas of hope. Greg's tumor is treatable, we live in the same city as one of the best brain tumor programs in the country, we have a deep support network, Greg doesn't need radiation or IV chemo – I'm sure there are more. Still, we are overwhelmed with the magnitude of all that has happened, the intense shift that our lives have taken, and the number of unknowns. There are no data on the long-term effects of using temozolomide – it is a new drug used for a variety of cancers.

Tuesday, Greg meets with the neurosurgeon for his post-op appointment. He hopes to get clearance to up his activity and to clarify a few things (like using the chain saw). The neurosurgeon is straight and to-the-point. He seems to understand Greg's way of navigating his disease, which has helped anchor Greg through overwhelming change.

Sometimes I try and put myself in Greg's place and imagine what it would feel like to have cancer cells in my brain. It's a strange place to go. My imagination can never capture what he is going through. Just as he was by my side through my pregnancies and childbirth, all I can really do is be by his side for this journey. I can't walk in his shoes, but I can create space in the day to talk, to let him know when I am afraid and when I am hopeful, to prepare his favorite dinner of beef and barley stew and then not get offended when he doesn't have the appetite to eat it and just wants to go to bed.

No Chemo (yet)

We are waiting for Greg's insurance to process his chemo. We will check in with the pharmacy tomorrow and see if there's anything we can do to move the bureaucracy along. We are waiting for an approval called "prior authorization", when the physician needs to complete paperwork explaining the patient's need for the medicine. Greg's paperwork has been completed and submitted, so we wait.

Last week, the MD said that she was starting Greg off on a higher dose than she usually does. Often, patients start at a lower dose and are titrated up over the first 2 - 3 cycles. Because Greg is so young and healthy, they want to skip the titration and start at the higher dose. Perhaps this is throwing off the insurance, but I don't know.

Weeks ago, during our preliminary meeting with the neurosurgeon, we first met his assistant in the Brain Tumor Center waiting area. He led us away from the clinic, through the winding hallways of the medical center, and up to the neurosurgeon's office in a wing of the medical school. We asked him what the plans were for a big construction project we walked past, and he said in a flat and steady tone, "I don't know. We'll find out by and by." That's how I feel about chemo right now – we'll find out, by and by.

And So It Begins

Greg's chemo medicine came in yesterday – 15 pills of cancer stomping fun. In case you were wondering, the movie Pootie Tang is a great stress reliever when starting chemo. Although, those of you who really know Greg would never doubt the stress reducing effects of such a fine cinematic masterpiece.

Day one down.

Greg also met with the neurosurgeon yesterday for his post-op appointment. The doctor gave him the all clear – running, biking, swimming, chainsawing are all OK. No driving. He did request that Greg not lose any fingers while using the chainsaw. He also suggested that Greg not go up onto the roof alone to do any repair work. He said that Greg could start feeling fatigue on day 3 of the pill cycle and this would last until 2 days after the end of the 5-day cycle. He encouraged Greg to exercise to help with the fatigue.

Greg (with some input from me) is strategizing his wish list of athletic events in the year ahead. He mailed in his registration for the 2012 Shut-in Ridge trail run – an 18 mile trail run in Asheville in early November that starts at the NC Arboretum and ends 2,800 feet higher at Mount Pisgah. This would be his 9th consecutive participation in the event. Most everything we've heard and read supports the benefits of exercise during cancer treatment. We even read about a woman who bicycled connected to her IV chemo pump.

Greg's starting chemo feels psychologically complex. In a way – it's great. Left unchecked, the cancer cells divide and divide and divide until the healthy body no longer functions. The fact that these pills exist, that people take them prevent cancer cells from dividing, is astounding. Still, the unknowns are overwhelming. The reality of the battle between devious DNA and pharmaceuticals is haunting, scary. The temozolomide is a critical piece of the equation. We also plan to dive into some of the more enjoyable parts of the cancer-fighting equation – getting enough sleep, spending time with people we love, telling jokes, praying, and other ways of cultivating joy.

Knowing

My best friend had serious complications during both of her pregnancies. In the 26th week of her second pregnancy, her obstetrician sent her to the hospital after a routine pregnancy visit. Even though my friend felt fine, her pregnancy assessment revealed some concerns. When she got to the hospital, the doctors evaluated her and her baby. They checked vital signs of mother and baby, drew bloodwork, and determined she was experiencing a severe, life threatening complication known as HELLP (hemolysis, elevated liver enzymes, and a low platelet count). The doctors said that she must deliver her baby immediately, via C-section.

She said "no."

She refused to let the doctors prep her for surgery. Every 15 minutes the doctors assessed her condition and insisted that she deliver the baby immediately. She still said "no." After a while of fruitless pleading, they switched to checking her every hour. They admitted her to the high-risk pregnancy floor. For days, they tried to convince her that she was putting her life and her baby's life in danger. They requested a psychological consult. The psychologist determined that my friend was perfectly sane.

My friend and her husband armed themselves with information about her condition. They demanded to speak with and solicit input from non-obstetrical specialists. They reviewed her labs and reports. My friend stayed on bedrest at the hospital for weeks and weeks. Eventually, her values improved and she was discharged home, still pregnant. The hospital had never discharged a pregnant woman home who was admitted with her condition.

My friend says that she knew that she did not need to deliver her baby. After the complications of her first pregnancy, she had learned about her pregnant body and about some of the ins-and-outs of navigating the health care system. She knew what it was like to deliver a baby weighing less than 2 pounds who needed to stay in the NICU for weeks. She knew that delivering a baby at 26 weeks could very well mean that she would leave the hospital alone or with a baby whose systems were not able to function at their best. Going against the medical advice of some of the most highly trained obstetricians in the world, she knew what was best for her and her baby.

Seven weeks after she was first sent to the hospital, 33-weeks into her pregnancy, my friend gave birth to a healthy, still premature baby boy. His delivery was brought on by a separate complication. She went back to the hospital knowing that it was time for her baby to come. She now has two healthy, beautiful sons who love and quarrel and drive her crazy and fill her life with immeasurable joy. What would her story be if she'd delivered at 26 weeks? When I think of her experience, I am struck by her powerful, innate knowing of what was right, even in the face of powerful forces telling her otherwise.

Since being diagnosed with cancer, Greg and I have come across several people who tell us that they know he is going to beat his cancer. When somebody says that they know he will get better, I am struck by a combination of guilt and skepticism. Why don't I possess this knowledge? How can they know such a thing? I very much want to know that Greg will overcome his cancer – that he will beat the odds, that there will come a time when the fears and worries of brain cancer are no longer present. I do not possess this knowledge right now.

The Brain Tumor Center motto is, "At Duke, There is Hope." Do I hope that Greg will get better? Absolutely. Do I know that there is a chance that he will be cancer free? Sure. However, my friend didn't hope that the doctors telling her to deliver at 26-weeks were wrong, she knew. Hoping and knowing are two very different things.

Attitude is an important ingredient in the recipe of healing. A little part of me worries that my not knowing that Greg will beat cancer is a chink in his healing armor. I worry about the future, about the possibility of the cancer's return, about how his body will respond to the chemo, about maybe needing radiation in the future. Are my worries the seeds of that which I fear? If I can banish these thoughts can I also banish the reality of what they represent?

Wisdom and experience tell me that while prayers, beliefs, attitudes, and knowledge are important parts of the healing process, they are not the only influencing factors. Many fearful, worried, hope-filled patients and families have traveled the cancer journey riddled with doubt, and walked through the other side cancer free. So have many determined, confident, knowing patients and families marched towards recovery, and had to say their goodbyes before they were ready.

As Greg's wife, I am grateful for the people around us who know that he will recover. They carry the impressive torch of unadulterated optimism. They are not distracted by doubt or fear or chance. For now, I still carry those distractions. For now, I carry the uncertainty of hope.

One Down, Eleven to Go

Greg finished his first chemo cycle. I feel ill-equipped to speak to how it went for him, since I wasn't the one taking the pills. Overall, he seemed to do OK through the 5-days. He described some of the expected symptoms, mainly fatigue and upset stomach. The low-point of his blood counts is supposed to be near day 21 of the cycle.

This weekend was much calmer than last – not nearly as much on our plates. Even so, the day-to-day activities are a challenge. Everything feels harder– making dinner, getting everybody ready and out the door for church, going through the evening bedtime routines. These mundane tasks feel Herculean. Our kids are wild, free, fierce, and full of energy. I am astounded by their passion for just about everything. Often, being around all of that energy makes me tired.

Who's Been Sleeping in My Bed?

In the week or so after surgery, Greg had trouble sleeping. What seemed most helpful with the frustration of insomnia was a good, lulling back scratch. I'm a good back scratcher for about 10 minutes, but then my arm gets tired and I am overcome by my own sleepiness. Eventually, as his wound healed and he came off the steroids, Greg's sleep returned. He still does favor a good back scratching before bed.

At Belle's school's open house the other night, the principal gave Greg a warm greeting and asked him to let her know if he needed anything. He was grateful for the offer. Later that night, somehow we got to joking that we should have said, "Yes, as a matter of fact, we need somebody who can come over and scratch Greg's back at bedtime for more than 10 minutes." The image of Belle's principal camped between us in bed, scratching his back while we both sleep, seemed pretty hilarious.

Like Greg's back scratcher, often, the help I want isn't practical or even possible. I need more hours in the day (or less sleep). I need my children to function for more than 10 minutes without me. I need to stop time completely so that I can just stop and breathe for a few moments. I need to know that the people I love are going to be OK. I need all these kooky gunmen who've been running wild and shooting people to just stop. I need the upcoming election to result in increased grace, compassion, and community and less fear, greed, and exclusion. I need drivers to stop speeding, tailgating, talking on their cell phones, and rolling through stop signs. See, in light of all of my needs, a night-time back scratcher seems pretty reasonable, yes?

Training

I often run around like a crazy person, getting worked up over the mechanics of getting through the day. I easily slide into the trap of trying to do everything and be everything. Greg is consistently the force of calm and humor. I look to him to tame the frenzy and find humor in the frustrations. Today, Greg and I were downstairs and we heard a loud "thud" – the kind of sound that no good can come from, especially when both children are out of sight. We wait a second, no screaming, crying, or laughing. We go upstairs to find that Abe had tried to scale Greg's wooden shelves that he keeps his clothes on and the whole thing had fallen over. As soon as he sees us, Abe promptly starts bawling. I was a bit worried that Abe was hurt – I've heard horror stories of children being crushed by shelves they were trying to climb. Greg quickly reasoned that Abe was OK, he was just stunned at what had happened. Greg and Abe stayed to put the shelves back up and replace the stacks of t-shirts, swim goggles and caps, and nick-knacks. I went back downstairs. There was no yelling, no fanfare, no more tears, no lost tempers.

Several times a week, Greg has found time during the day to put on his running shoes and head out the door for a run. I am proud that he is getting out and running, proud that he is pushing himself, and proud that he is not pushing too hard or getting worked up over the details of pace, distance, heart rate, etc. As he returns to the familiar rhythm of hips guiding knees guiding feet, I sense that he is happy to be moving, building, and getting into the rhythm of exercise again.

Greg starts back to work tomorrow. He has learned the bus system and has friends who have offered to help with rides. With a letter from the Brain Tumor Center, he got a disability bus pass that cuts the cost of the fares in half. I will be in charge of the kid transport and Greg seems to be doing well (and even enjoying) working the bus system, along with his bike and a borrowed scooter.

Bloodwork

The first round of Greg's bloodwork didn't seem particularly noteworthy. His platelet counts dropped, but are still within the normal range. The Band-Aid clinging to the crook of his arm sits as a reminder of cancer cells hiding within the folds of his cerebral cortex.

Greg is figuring out the logistics of fitting the lab visit into his work and family schedule. This time, he biked to a lab near our house and then biked to work. He learned that the computer at the main check-in desk isn't connected to the lab. He sat and waited at the lab for a long while before he realized that he needed to check in again at the lab. He gets his blood checked again on Monday and will start the next cycle of chemo on Monday or Tuesday.

The oncology RN went ahead and called in Greg's next chemo cycle. Abe and I went to the cancer center on Friday to pick up the prescription before getting Belle from school. The pharmacist greeted Abe with a wide, welcoming smile. With no words spoken, she knows that Abe is learning to understand his Dad's disease, that traveling to the cancer center is part of his journey with the Wild Things. Abe and I leave the goose-bump producing air conditioning of the medical world into the humid, early fall air. With thousands of dollars of chemotherapy tucked into my backpack, we blend into the bustle of the afternoon and head to the car to pick up Belle.

Holy Crap, I Married a Super Hero!

We are now a one car family. Greg sold our clunker soon after surgery – a 2-door, stick-shift Nissan from the early 1990s. He figured that he wouldn't be driving for a while and wanted extra cash on hand. So far, having only one car has been easy. However, I get zero brownie points for experiencing much of an inconvenience on my part – Greg is doing most of the grunt work. As he walks to the bus stop, flashing his disability pass to the driver and dropping two quarters into the fare meter; as he bikes from home to the lab to work; as he throws his backpack into the trunk of a co-worker's car and slides into the passenger seat, Greg could be the poster child for suburban commuting using non-single driver means.

Today, I was humbled and amazed as he left the house with the morning light. He biked from home to the lab for bloodwork; then to work and back home again towing our bike trailer with clothes, lunches for the week, computer, and backpack. This is a man who had a craniotomy on July 11th and has been through one round of chemotherapy. Oh, and somewhere along the way he stopped by a machine shop to get a spare chain for his chainsaw. Is this guy for real?

The oncology RN reviewed Greg's bloodwork and decided to postpone his next round of chemo for a few days. His values went down instead of up, and he can't start cycle two until his blood counts start trending upwards again. He was bummed because he wants to be done with chemo ASAP. I am bummed for him, but also glad that the doctors and nurses are keeping such a close watch on him. He'll get his blood checked again on Friday and will likely start cycle two when these results are on. His spirit way buoyed when he went to the mailbox and found his acceptance into the 2012 Shut-In Ridge run.

Hanging

We have begun to settle into the rhythm of fall. As the day comes to an end, dark arrives earlier than in summertime. Abe and Belle are in school. Greg and I are working. Mornings are cooler. Hints of yellow, orange, and brown dull the summer's vibrant green. The anticipation of the coming holidays is beginning to mummer at the edges of our consciousness. Who will be what for Halloween? How might the weather be for our Thanksgiving beach time? There are even a few, somewhat predictable moments during the week when I am home alone and able to make dinner, tame some of the constant clutter, and read one of my mom's People magazines.

Through the clutter and chaos, our world is still filled with love. I awoke this morning around 5:15a and went for a short jog. The lights were blazing at our neighbor's house across the street. I ran into another neighbor out walking her dogs. Part of me knows that no reasonable human should be up and functioning at this hour. Still, I was comforted by my neighbors out braving the world with me in the dark.

Am I Going to Die?

Greg had a follow-up blood draw today as his medical team tries to pin down the nadir of his blood counts. The RN just contacted him and said that his platelets dropped just a small amount again, so no chemo yet. He'll do another blood draw on Monday. The RN also said that there is flexibility in the timing of the chemo, and that she does not worry about a 1-week delay.

During a car ride, Abe asks, "Am I going to die?" Hmmmm, that's a tough one. I don't remember our exact words in response, but they were something along the lines of "Well, everybody dies eventually, but you don't need to worry about that right now." Abe starts hysterically sobbing "I don't want to die, I don't want to die." Shit. Belle tried to comfort Abe, but she couldn't come up with words that made sense to him. At one point, she was running around the house singing "It's OK Abe, when you die, you fly!!" She may have been thinking of dying and going to heaven. This only made Abe more upset.

I don't know that Greg and I have ever had a concrete conversation about how to discuss death with our children. I want to acknowledge death without creating an overwhelming sense of anxiety or fear. With Belle, I ended up telling her that death comes for those who are really, really old or really, really sick. Since she is neither of these things, she does not need to worry about dying. Since his tears in the car ride home from the puppet show, we have tried to reinforce this message to Abe.

It has still come up a couple of times, though. Later he asked again "Am I going to die?" Our conversation went along these lines:

Me: *No, you are not going to die. Are you really, really old?*

Abe: *No.*

Me: *Are you really, really sick?*

Abe: *No.*

Me: *Then you're OK.*

Another time this week, Abe asked, "Is Daddy still very sick?" I said that he is sick, but that he is not very, very sick. I explained that he is going to doctors and taking medicine to help him get better. Abe seemed OK with that.

Milestones – September 16, 2012

We hit a big milestone this weekend – Abe relinquished his pacifiers, "binkis", and marched into the land of Big Boys. As with Belle, we took him to the Build-a-Bear store at our local mall. He selected a royal blue bear with white stars. He placed his assortment of binkis into the bear and then a staff member filled the bear with white, polyester stuffing and a small cloth heart, stitching him up. Abe shed a few tears the day prior to going to the mall – "I don't WANT to put my binkis in a bear. I am NOT a big boy." However, he did surprisingly well at the store, with not a tear shed, showing more excitement than sadness.

Abe was pretty bummed at bedtime, with more tears and declarations of wanting his binkis back and not wanting to be a big boy. We offered him lots of hugs and sympathy and told him he'd get through these tough times. It was cute, and also sad. We are officially a diaper-free, binky-free household.

Cycle Two

The third time was a charm for Greg's blood draws. His blood counts were slow to bounce back after the first cycle of chemo. After his third blood draw in 8 days, he finally got the go-head to start his second cycle of chemo last evening. Let's hope that the drug is as tough on the cancer cells as it was on his platelets.

He takes anti-nausea medication before the chemo and he is also still on his anti-seizure meds. Tonight, at bedtime, we wished we had some anti-temper tantrum meds in the house for Belle and Abe. Abe was hysterical over giving up his pacifiers. As I was reading him his bedtime stories, he keep pointing to each character in the book saying, "He's mean, and he's mean, and he's mean … ." Belle was hysterical over Abe's behavior and frustration over trying to read "Bear's Loose Tooth." Fortunately, Greg and I were able to keep it together, and both kids were tucked snugly into their beds at a reasonable hour.

I continue to be so very proud of Greg. He is fully participating in helping keep our household intact, he is immersing himself in fatherhood, and he is working full time. It is an honor to bear witness to his strength and patience.

Toys

We are a low-tech household. Greg does not own a cell phone and mine is a plain, pre-paid one that I almost never use. We have an old TV, salvaged from a friend who was transitioning to the world of flat-screens. Our TV is hooked up to a DVD and nothing else – no cable or satellite or whatever else is out there to bring media into your home. Greg and I share a laptop. We don't have a microwave.

A couple of weeks ago, a friend sent Greg an iTouch. As I have been coveting a digital device like this for a while (a tablet, actually, if you must know), Greg very generously offered to let me take control of the new digital device. I declined, knowing that the person who sent it intended it for Greg. It is even engraved with a beloved nickname "The Greatest American Sousa."

After some initial reticence, Greg dove into his new toy with the zest and zeal of an engineer. It is fun to watch him integrate it into little aspects of his daily life. He's not obsessed (he's much more fixated on sharp devices used to cut down and split trees). However, he uses it daily. We are stealing wireless access from our neighbor (with permission). When discussing upcoming plans, he whips out the iTouch and pulls up the date in question to let me know what is going on. He loads in birthdays and running events, checks e-mail and the weather, and downloads music. He's even put in this cycle of chemo-dates and when he needs to get the blood draws done. I don't see him getting into any fancy apps, since he won't want to pay for them, but he is tapping into whatever free resources are out there. I see the appeal of these types of digital devices – they're convenient, hold lots of information, and yes, they're fun! I just feel sooo 21st century.

On a different topic, this round of chemo seems much like the last. He has a bit of stomach upset, but nothing that he complains about. He is generally more tired than before his seizure in June – he conks out earlier in the evening and doesn't bounce out of bed quite as early in the morning. However, the basic day-to-day flow of our lives is very much the same. We're going to and from work, brushing teeth (big and small), trying our best to prepare healthy meals, reading bedtime stories, and spending time outdoors enjoying the transition to fall. Belle and Abe picked out their Halloween costumes – a fox for Belle and Batman for Abe. After shopping at the mall, I decided to order the costumes on-line. Every day, the kids practically jump out of their skin waiting for the mail to come.

Greg is slowly building for the race in November. Because he can't drive, he's finagling ways to get to and from some of his favorite running spots. Last weekend, the four of us went to Umstead park. Greg ran 8 miles while the kids and I hiked the bike and bridle trails. Tomorrow, he has plans to meet up with running buddies for a 10-mile run at Duke Forest. I'm looking forward to visiting the farmer's market tomorrow – local pecans are calling my name, and fresh ginger is in season.

Balance

The day after Greg's last chemo pill was the fall equinox. In addition to beginning one of the most glorious seasons here in NC, it is also a unique day of the year when daylight and darkness are roughly equal. I'm not sure if the equinox really holds much importance from an astronomical perspective, but culturally, it represents a balance between light and dark. There was much about this past weekend that felt more balanced to me than in weeks past.

Wee Snuggles

I think about what has changed since Greg's cancer diagnosis. Now that we are past the scary, insane, intense days and weeks after his seizure and surgery and diagnosis, many aspects of our lives have returned to normal (or "baseline", as they like to say in the medical world). Greg and I are each working, the kids are in school, we fill our weekends with fun activities (often something athletic), we try and stay connected with friends and family, and Greg still says atop of our toilet paper supply. However, when people ask, "Are things back to normal?", I find that I struggle to answer "yes."

I was never drawn to the parenting practice of co-sleeping. There is a raging debate about the pros and cons of baby-parent bed sharing. While the American Academy of Pediatrics is strongly against it, I happen to know that an epidemiologist who helped monitor and track the SIDS database at the CDC co-slept with her infant. She knew how to bring her little one safely into her bed – free from excess bedding and pillows, with no pre-bed alcohol consumption, her baby could safely sleep by her side, free to nurse with minimal disruption. As an anxious, stressed-out new mom, throwing an infant into our bed didn't feel right to me. Belle and Abe each slept in a bassinet next to our bed for the first couple of months. Once the nighttime feedings settled down a bit, we moved them into their own crib and room.

When Belle was a toddler, she ended up sleeping in our bed with us on occasion. It may have started as part of a travel trip, where the number of people and beds were such that it just made sense to bed share. Once Abe was born, the home-based co-sleeping stopped. Not so much by intent, it just seemed to happen.

Over the past few weeks, Belle has found her way back into our bed. Abe has caught on. We're not crazy enough to try and wrangle the four of us into one bed. However, often on the weekend, each child takes a turn snuggling between us for the night. They get so excited about the prospect of sleeping in our bed. They'll even ask about it during the week, "Daddy, can I sleep in your bed tonight?" "Not tonight, wait until the weekend."

Whatever reservations I had about co-sleeping when the children were infants are gone. Yes, there are many nights when it just doesn't make sense to have a little one in bed with us (like when my alarm is set to go off at 5:15a so that I can get in a run). However, without discussing it much, Greg and I look forward to a weekend evening of a family slumber party. I sleep well on the nights when Belle or Abe are next to me. Greg says the same. A small, warm body tucks in between us, as their breath settles from the day. They are relaxed and at peace and so clearly content and nurtured. During the night, a little hand or foot will find its way over onto me. If it's uncomfortable, I gently move it back. Otherwise, I enjoy the warmth of their little limb and then drift back to sleep myself. Given how much has changed in our lives over the past months, these moments of quiet calm during the night are nurturing.

Our family bed-sharing nights will not last. The kids will get older and bigger and lose interest. Or, Greg and I will realize that the dynamics are no longer nurturing or healthy. Until then, we will enjoy an evening here and there with a mama and a papa and a little one safely snuggled together.

Winter Teaser

A cool front is passing through our area. Not even a cold front, since the low is still a robust 54 degrees. We were visited by a booming thunder storm last night (which I completely slept through) and most of the day was cool and rainy. When he awoke this morning, Greg received a message from his wood-splitting-partner-in-crime, Drew, saying that a large oak had fallen in a neighbor's yard. After going for a 12-mile run in the morning, Greg went and helped his friend split the fallen oak for winter fuel. Greg reports feeling great on his run – he and a running buddy did four circuits of a 3-mile loop. His last circuit was faster than his first – known as a negative split in the running world. He feels like Shut-In is within reach.

We'd originally talked about going to a pumpkin patch in the afternoon, but the abundance of rain made those plans seem less-than-ideal. Instead, we loaded up the kids and went with friends to our local children's museum. After playing for a couple of hours, the grown-ups' stomachs started to grumble, and we agreed to head over to a local BBQ joint. Lots of turkey, ribs, mac-and-cheese, onion rings, beef brisket, hamburger, and baked beans later, our bellies were filled and all was well. Oh – we sealed the deal with some Blue Bell ice cream, yumm!

When we got home, I worked as my own sous-chef for a batch of gumbo and some oatmeal, pumpkin muffins I'm hoping to assemble tomorrow. The kids watched a movie, and Greg channeled the energy from the day and built a fire in our woodstove. We had to open the porch doors to achieve a comfortable temp, but it was still fun. We may cook like little Sousa pigs-in-a-blanket this evening, but it's nice to get a taste of winter to come. Our poor family members from the north come to visit us in the winter and get roasted by our woodstove. But, us wimpy southern folk love to have one awesomely cozy room in the house during the winter.

Germs (and unexpected blessings)

I am not a "germ person." I do not own Lysol, I try and steer clear of antibacterial soap and go for the regular stuff, I'm OK if Belle and Abe are playing with somebody with a cough or runny nose, and Greg is usually the one who reminds the kids to wash their hands before dinner and after using the bathroom. I know enough about germs to be reasonable – I support basic hand hygiene and do my best to keep Belle and Abe away from people with fevers, vomiting, contagious rashes and more serious ailments.

A side effect of chemotherapy is immunosuppression. In addition to targeting rapidly dividing cancer cells, the chemo also targets rapidly dividing blood cells including red and white blood cells and platelets. Since white blood cells fight infection, when white cell counts go down, so does the body's ability to fight germs.

Since Greg's started chemo, I've made a couple of changes in my approach to germs. For work, I usually visit patients in their homes, and sometimes I'll see them in the hospital. Either way, I come across some nasty germs like MRSA and c-diff – I have more than a handful of patients with these infections. I used to leave my work shoes just inside our front door. However, if my arms were loaded with groceries or children or the like, I would just wear my shoes into the house and change them later. Now, I change my work shoes in the car, leaving them in a closed bag, and put on non-work shoes before coming into the house. If Greg is exposed to one of the nastier germs out there, the consequences could land him in the hospital, as opposed to on the couch with tea and soup.

I am also giving more thought to this year's influenza vaccine. I got this year's flu shot last week at work. For the past couple of years, I had Belle and Abe get the flu-mist influenza vaccine. This is a live, attenuated virus that is squirted into the nose. Belle and Abe find the nose-squirt infinitely preferable to the needle.

This year, the wee ones need the old-fashioned shot. Because the nose squirt contains a live virus, Greg is technically more susceptible to getting sick from the weakened virus. Getting the flu shot is one little thing I can do to maybe, possibly keep our crew healthier this winter and spring.

Planning

I am a planner. If you casually mention to me that we should do lunch sometime, within 4 seconds, I've figured out what day will work best, where we should eat, who will sit where, what I will wear, and what to order. Give me 4 more seconds, and I'll have Google mapped the most efficient way to get to our destination. Heck, I'll even throw in the weather forecast for free! Knowing what lies ahead reduces my anxiety.

Lately, my planning well is running dry. Every month, I do our family calendar that maps our work schedules, school schedules, trips, races, birthday parties, medical appointments, and the like. I started including Greg's chemo cycle, bloodwork, and oncology appointments, but after the first cycle, we quickly learned that the dates are not fixed – influenced by things beyond our control. His appointments get changed, cancelled, rescheduled, again and again. We are learning to accept this as part of life with cancer. Even with Greg putting some dates in his iTouch, I still need pen and paper to keep all of our activities together (plus, Greg is likely to not keep up with the birthday of one of the kids' classmates).

My tolerance for any additional planning is depleted. I used to feel invigorated coordinating weekends away and social events with friends and family. Now, I get overwhelmed and grumpy. I can mostly manage the day-to-day details of our four lives, but not much else. People look to me as the Queen Planner of the house, like they've always done, and I look back with a scowl and a sigh. They mean no ill-intent and I know that none is intended.

Somewhere in my current planning angst is a life lesson. Living in the moment is touted as one of the sacred keys to true happiness. Planning and living in the moment aren't exactly incompatible, but it doesn't take much for them to cancel each other out. Be here now. Not yesterday. Not tomorrow. But now.

Last weekend, as I was putting Belle to bed, she asked what we were doing the next day. I told her that I wasn't sure. She kept asking and I kept finding different ways to tell her that I didn't know. Eventually, she told me that she had a stomachache because she was worried that we didn't have set plans for the following day. I explained that we're not always going to know what the next day brings, and sometimes it's fun to wake-up and decide. She skeptically rolled over for her back scratch. Hopefully, her little spirit will learn the gifts that can come from the unknown, the unplanned, and the unscheduled. Hopefully, the same can be said for me.

Troublesome Trucks

There is an episode of Thomas and Friends with characters called "the Troublesome Trucks." They are a couple of trucks that misbehave and disrupt the flow of life in the Island of Sodor, causing angst and consternation for the other generally well behaved trains and trucks. Greg and I sometimes refer to things in our day-to-day life as 'troublesome trucks'. We might say, "There was a troublesome truck at the science museum today who gave Belle some grief while we were watching the lemurs." Or, "Grrrrr, the internet is being a troublesome truck, I can't get it to connect."

For the past week, Greg's right calf has been a troublesome truck. He pushed his body during run a little over a week ago. A couple of days after that, he went for a short run at work and his calves seized up on him. Ever since, his right calf has been sore. I gave him a calf massage the first night and it felt like somebody had shoved clumps of mud under his skin. His muscles have loosened up somewhat, but that right calf is still a wee bit sore.

Unfortunately, having this pain is changing his running rhythm. He knows how to listen to his body and rest when needed. He still has a few weeks to train for the run in Asheville, but we're getting worried that he won't have the foundation he needs to make it up the mountain. Our back-up plan all along has been that Greg would serve as a race volunteer if he was unable to run. We knew that running 18 miles up a mountain a mere 4 months after a craniotomy was pretty ambitious. However, we also thought that if he couldn't do the run, it would be because of the surgery or the cancer treatment, not a calf strain. I can't help but think that his body is tapped, and that the calf soreness is indirectly related to everything his body has been through.

Hopefully, his troublesome truck will settle down and he can continue to build his long runs over the next few weeks. Given everything he's been through, switching from running to volunteering isn't a big deal. Still, there is a good amount of psychological pride in pushing through the difficulties to meet a challenge. I'm still envisioning him doing the race – sometimes running, sometimes walking, but still crossing the finish line with a sense of pride and accomplishment.

Rhythms

Our family has been shaped by Belle and Abe's Waldorf preschool. The teachers often talk about rhythm – daily, weekly, and seasonal rhythms. A rhythm is similar to a schedule, without the formal structure and confines. The children know what to expect without being hung up by the rigidity us grown-ups often need to traverse our days.

This week, Family Sousa's rhythm of has been a bit off. Heading to work on Monday, Greg found that his bike had a flat tire. He changed the tube but needed to run an extra errand to get a new tube and tire, and got to work late. Tuesday, he went to school Mass with Belle. Going to Tuesday Mass gives Greg an anchor of calm and connectedness to Belle, but it also means that he gets to work late (he walks from Belle's school to the downtown bus terminal, where he then catches a bus to work). Today, Greg had a blood draw, which he biked to before heading off to work. Tomorrow, he is volunteering at Belle's school in the morning for Hispanic Heritage week. Friday, we hope to go out with my MT Dad and step-Mom, who are visiting from Montana. Greg very much wants to be at home in the evenings to be with family, but he also has a full plate at work. He's generally been coming home between 7p and 8p. I do my best to transition the kids from school to home, help Belle with her homework, keep Abe from damaging himself or others, and feed them. I've said this before and I'll say it again – I am always so happy to see Greg's face when he arrives home.

We are still getting used to the nuances of Greg's chemo schedule. Last week, the oncology RN said that his bloodwork "looks great." Today, he went in for his 2nd blood draw of the cycle, hoping to start his 3rd cycle of chemo. He is still planning on running the race in Asheville, and wants as many days as possible between chemo and the race, for his stomach to settle down. When he e-mailed the RN about picking up his chemo, she said to wait until after his MRI and oncology appointment, which is scheduled for October 25th. So – round three of chemo is on hold. Those of you who have already been on this cancer journey in one way or another are likely smiling a knowing smile or nodding a knowing nod. You've already been here before. We are now getting clued in.

Through the disruptions, my uber-planning self seeks out the rhythm. This week is off-kilter, but there are reminders of the natural pulse of life. We've started fires in our stove when the nights dip into the 40s. While some of our rhythms have been disrupted, the ones that are still present provide a much needed anchor to the comfort of friends, family, and the seasons of this orb we call home.

You Know it's Bad ...

... when I go to make banana chocolate chip muffins and there are no chocolate chips in the house. I assembled all of the batter, heated the oven, greased the muffin tins, and reached into the cabinet for my trusty bag of chips. Which was not to be found. Anywhere. Nor was there a back-up bag. Ohhhh, I was bummed. So, after a few minutes of frantic searching, I reached for the cocoa powder instead and dumped a bunch in. One batch of banana chocolate muffins later, all was right with the world.

The other thing that has gone missing is Greg's platelets. On day 21 of his blood draw they were 206,000. On day 30, they were 105,000. Chemo cannot be given if the platelets are lower than 100,000. We were already on hold until his MRI next week, but we seem to be learning that the nadir for Greg's bloodwork is closer to day 30 of the cycle than day 21. Next week, we'll see what the oncologist says about how this affects the 12 cycles we were thinking would happen.

Tomorrow, Greg is going for a long run, his calf is feeling much better.

Community

While out and about yesterday, Greg stopped at a yard with a felled, segmented tree. This scene screams "free winter heat!!" On our way to church today, we stopped to leave a note at the house, to ask about taking some of the wood. The homeowner was home, so he and Greg talked a bit about felling large trees and firewood and burning for winter heat. While they were talking, the wife walked outside to join us – a beautiful women wearing a rather striking shirt with a black and white image of Audrey Hepburn. She recognized Greg as somebody she comes across while bike commuting to work. Before stopping our car, the members of this household were complete strangers to us. After just a few moments, connections were made over firewood and bike communing. By the end of the day, we had a front lawn piled high with winter heat.

Cycle Three

Greg's appointments at the cancer center on Thursday went well. The punch line is that his MRI scan shows that his tumor shaped like a finger is shrinking and another spot of concern is completely gone, yeah!

The day included a blood draw, MRI, meeting with oncology team, and pharmacy stop for chemo pick-up. We got to all of Greg's appointments early and he was seen either early or on-time. His bloodwork showed that his blood counts are back up, so he got the green light for his third cycle of chemo. He fell asleep in the MRI for the first time and twitched a bit, so they had to retake one of the images. The images are uploaded into his medical record so that the oncologist can review them right away.

At the oncologist's office, we first met the PA with whom we struggled a bit at the last visit. This time, Greg didn't crack any jokes and the visit was much smoother. Not everybody can appreciate Greg's sense of humor. Greg enjoys making his oncology team laugh (or at least smile) and they seem to love his spirit and energy, so on the whole, we feel well cared for and understood by the brain tumor group. The PA did the usual battery of neuro checks – simple tests of balance, peripheral vision, math, and memory. We reviewed his chemo dates, which seem to cause some confusion because Greg's blood counts don't follow the expected pattern of a low on day 21 and a rebound by day 28. He trends about 3 days behind. The oncologist does not suggest that there is any concern regarding this pattern. Greg gets positive feedback for his exercise and his super-fantastic blood pressure and heart rate.

It is unsettling to look at pictures of Greg's brain flashing across the computer screen. He's had 5 scans from initial diagnosis, through surgery, and now 2 months into chemo. The cavity left by the tumor the surgeons removed is filled with cerebral spinal fluid and the surgical borders are healed. There were two notable pieces of tumor left after surgery – one that looked like a small clumpy blob along the surgical edge and another longer, thinner piece extending away from the main tumor like a little finger or arm. On this scan, the little blobby thing was gone, and the finger extension was notably thinner and smaller.

The goal is that Greg will get the all-clear after a year of treatment. The oncologist said that after the year of chemo, he will get an MRI every 2 months for a year, every 3 months the next year, every 4 months for a year, then every 6 months for a year. After two clean 6-month scans, he transitions to yearly MRIs for the rest of his life. We understand that this plan is textbook and that unknown factors can influence what actually happens. Still, my planning, analytical self likes to at least have a sense of expectations, knowing that life is strange and unpredictable.

Our last stop was at the pharmacy. We seek out the same pharmacist each time, asking for her by name. We chatted and learned about her plans for her 50th birthday. She initially thought that she wanted to go to Europe with her husband. She changed her mind and is instead going to Georgia (USA) to visit a charity she supports. She reflected that instead of spending a bunch of money to "get a notch on my belt" she wants to share her blessings with people in need. It was a wonderful way to end our day at the cancer center. During the days ahead Greg will finish this cycle of chemo and rest up for our trip to Asheville.

In Greg's Words

Before Shut In Trip – November 1, 2012

This is Greg writing. When did I become a survivor? Was it upon diagnosis which would be July 2012. Or was it at the unknown time of inception of the tumor some many years ago? Regardless, I have always been a survivor and will move forward that way.

After the July 11, 2012 surgery and recovery Sara and I talked about a lot of things, and we still do now, when we have time. One item was the annual pilgrimage to Asheville NC for the Shut In Ridge Trail Run (SIRTR). Oddly I learned that SIRTR existed while running the Bridger Ridge Run north of Bozeman, MT in August 2003, go figure. Getting into SIRTR is difficult since just over 200 runners are allowed to participate but more than that send in registration. Since I have completed 8 before the brain tumor bit me I was guaranteed an entry to SIRTR for 2012.

The conversation lasted about 2 weeks. We had to deliberate if I could safely regain sufficient fitness to safely complete the event on November 03, 2012, 4 months after surgery. We had no problem committing to going to the event the decision point was whether I would run or volunteer. Volunteering would afford me the opportunity to still be involved in the event, give back, and sort of keep the streak. Our ending decision was to not decide. I signed up for the event to reserve my place on the list. Sara as always was unwavering in her support of our ambition to have me run. Later after some time of training I would make the decision to run or volunteer.

The first 3 weeks of rebuilding were unlike any rebuilding I have experienced before in my athletic life. Humbling to say the least and reaffirming my continual sense of appreciation, I do not just mean athletics. Finally I broke through, sort of.

I focused my rebuilding of long runs at the Al Buehler trail. I am vaguely aware of the credible reputation he has left as well as being aware that he was at 3 or 4 Olympics on the coaching staff. The Buehler trail is close to home while also topographically challenging. I was quite fortunate to have a friend I used up repeatedly in this running rebuilding process for these long runs. We are paced near enough to each other and I am not allowed to drive yet. I owe her big time. My breakthrough when I believed I could march/run SIRTR 2012 came on September 29, 2012. Our plan was to run 3 laps at Buehler trail together on September 29, 2012. It had rained a lot that night and the morning was still with mist, some drizzle. The temperature was fine while running. Perhaps near the middle or end of our second loop it started to rain and it continued to rain the remaining time we were out there. At the end of 3 loops together we stopped for her to get her bike and she biked the 4th loop while I ran it. I was well aware that biking would drop her body heat compared to running and the rain was not stopping, I was humbled with appreciation again. During this 4th loop is when my internal voice told me I could try and march/run SIRTR this year. It was a moment.

Sara has been the biggest supporter of me and the family. Through this cancer blip and also since the inception of family. My gratitude is large.

I write this post on November 01, 2012, my first attempt at running a marathon was November 01, 1992.

On we go to try SIRTR in 2012, for my ninth running. Sara's favorite number is 9.

GDS Writing After Shut In. My Body Covered the Distance, But it was Sara's Spirit

November 01, 1992 was my first attempt at a marathon and so far my only DNF (Did Not Finish). I wrote a pre- Shut In post to this blog on November 01, 2012, aware of the date. I had no expectation of DNF at Shut In this year, but I was cautious. We learned the day before the race that an extra mile was being tacked on, bringing the total distance to 19 miles. My training was suspect to say the least, given my circumstance, so having to accept the addition of a mile did not matter.

Leonard and Mary Anna joined us this year in Asheville. They have been a huge part of this journey too. We stayed at the hotel with our Durham friends from Carolina Godiva. We were in room number 318. Which, thanks to Blake for the realization, was Belle's birthday, March 18.

Event day was Sa Nov. 03, 2012. The weather was nice with clear skies and 50s/60s for air temperature. We had breakfast at the hotel and headed over to the NC Arboretum at 9:00a. As usual the arboretum is a fantastic place to be, race or no race. We got to connect with John and Kathy Nichols, this is the ninth consecutive time that we have entered this event. We saw a lot of our Durham friends from Carolina Godiva.

I wore my CamelBak water bladder to carry over one and a half liters of water. I also carried six gel packs. I could not allow any space for me running out of drink or calories while I was out there for what I expected to be a long day. The race started at 10:00a and I paired up with Shawn as I have done for the last 2 or 3 editions of Shut In. Shawn was doing a charity service for me and stayed with me for 75 minutes, too long for him. I was glad he did as I enjoy his company. The first 75 minutes were fine. I can admit to having a few thoughts of wondering how my body would be in 1 hour, in 2 hours, etc. At 75 minutes in I finally got Shawn to leave me.

I ran alone for a few miles before getting to Bent Creek. However at this point in the event there were still people near enough ahead and behind that I had awareness of others. It was a neat section because I was alone and not speaking with others. I am not sure I have been alone for that section of the course before. The weather, the leaves, and the views of the forest from within.

I made it to the Bent Creek aid station. This is about 10 miles into the course, around halfway of the course distance but mentally perhaps the beginning of the race. I stopped there and spoke with Kathy a little bit. I had been trying to get a good drink at every aid station. Kathy said John had come on through some time ago and looked good. Next up was Ferrins Knob, I planned to walk the ascent. I ended up pairing with Rose whom I originally met at Shut In 2011. Rose was running with her friend Nova. We had a woman pass us at the beginning of this climb, Rose recognized her as Abby. Days later in my neighborhood I learned that my friend Ilana was friends with Abby and knew she was at Shut In. Perhaps some other time I will meet Abby.

I had met Rose at Shut In 2011 when I was paired with Shawn. This year Rose overtook us early in the race. While I was with her for the beginning climb of Ferrins Knob I did not expect to stay with her. This was the first time I walked the entire climb of Ferrins Knob and it was nice. It is a slow grade for a good portion and then it ramps up. We were talking through this climb. The descent from the top is steep and tricky. We popped out at an aid station on the Blue Ridge Parkway and I saw a couple of friends at the aid station. One in particular had my attention because of the decision she had to make. She and her husband were set to run the race. They had kidcare lined up for their young children. However, as the start of the race drew near the children became unsettled. It was enough to make her decide not to race. There she was, bib pinned to her clothes, months of preparation, logistics made; and she made the decision of family. When I saw her at that aid station I tried to convey respect and sympathy to her without saying so directly. I know that conflict well and I respect and applaud her decision. Also at that aid station was another friend who came down with sickness just before Shut In. She had to change her plan and slow down her run.

Coming out of that aid station I let go of Rose and decided to stay with Karen who was feeling sick. I liked the prospect of having someone to run with and did not want to impose myself too much on one person. This seemed to work and Karen and I did well to chat. We separated and I ran ahead a little. I caught back up to Rose and others and formed a bunch, but Nova had left Rose. We stayed like that for another chunk of time. Karen joined us too. Our bunch started to separate with Rose falling off the back. I was aware of her condition so I did not try to stay with Karen. Eventually it was just Rose and I as the race was thinned out. We popped out on to the Blue Ridge Parkway again, but nothing. This was one of the aid stations of years past which was now empty. Since the Blue Ridge Parkway was also closed for this section there was not even someone there to act as a crossing guard. It was surreal to walk across this pavement with only another competitor, it was quiet and beautiful. No cars moving or parked and the vista was simply hanging there for us. We paused too, uncertain of where to pick the trail back up again.

Back on the trail we started to do more walking and Rose was having a tough time. She could not ingest drinks or gels. It worked out well for me as we were over 3 hours in and I knew I needed to stay conservative. The longest run I had done in training was just over 2 hours and none of my preparation was good enough for the terrain of Shut In. So we walked and walked. We got to a decision point though. The Highway 151 aid station has a cut-off time of 4 hours. I knew I was going to complete the course and for personal and family reasons it was very important that I achieve this goal. I could observe that Rose was suffering a lot and if someone does have a hard time on the trail it could be some time before the next person comes by and could offer help. Rose and I talk through this and we decide it is time for me to move on. At 3 hours and 50 minutes on the race clock I began to run again`and I made it to the Highway 151 aid station at 3:54. Rose made it to Highway 151 and prudently chose to DNF.

At the Highway 151 aid station I stopped as I have done the 7 times previously to say hello and thank you to Bob Cutler. Bob had run 25 Shut In races with his last one being my first, 2004. I was at that aid station with Joe and we begin the ascent together. It is approximately 2 miles from this aid station to the old finish and approximately 3 miles to the new finish. I like to refer to this aid station as the halfway point in the psychological race because the next portion of climbing is the hardest. Joe and I stay together for this whole climb, walking the majority. At the crest I take Shawn's advice and pull off the course for a spectacular view. It was worth it. As we neared the end of the trail part of the course, I finally fell. I had been concerned about falling because I had hurt my ribs a second time one week before Shut In. It was the kind of fall I have thought about from time to time on the Shut In course through the years but never suffered before. In short, I fell to my back and rolled, sort of. No problem with the ribs. Joe, bless his heart, checked up to see if I was okay. Then we came off the trail, at the old finish. This too was surreal since I have memories from 8 past editions of hearing the crowd before seeing them and on this day we heard nothing. Then out of the trail we see a race clock, but there is no timer, no volunteer, no one. In fact this parking lot was also closed to the public. Again, another experience of surreal beauty, quiet and calm amidst the exertion of a difficult event. The last mile is pavement. I needed to be done. I hit the old finish line at 4:36 and I speculated I might finish at the new finish line by 4:30, I knew Sara was waiting. I paced myself well through the first 18 miles, walked a lot, I ran the last mile comfortably.

I got about one hundred meters before the finish line and I saw folks. Sara, Belle, Abe, Beme, Papi, Family Esselstyn, John, Kathy, and Carolina Godiva friends! I made it, a big deal. I paused to take it in. The children ran to me, held my hand and showed me a congratulations poster board. I tried to get the three children to walk in with me over the finish line. Abe had no interest after the initial greeting, he was busy stomping snow. Belle and Hattie walked with me holding hands. However, as we got closer to the finish line and Hattie got further from her dad, she said she wanted to go be with her dad (cute!).
One of the many neat parts of Shut In is the stained glass award for a top 20 finish. While that has never been feasible for me, I did get a different award this year in addition to the poster. Hattie made a bead bracelet and presented it to me around a can which held flowers.

Eating after multi-hour athletic events is usually an adventure for me. I am beyond tired and want good nutrition. At the same time I want to load my belly with ribs for example, but I know such a choice would actually lock my belly for too long. I want the food to get in, flow past the stomach and be rich in replenishment. I am fortunate to have done many multi-hour events in my life through these years. After this Shut In I had my first opportunity to explore food intake in a way that clicked. Shortly after the event, during the car ride down from the ridgeline I ate Dahl thanks to Cindy. Awesome taste and wonderful nutrification from lentils. Next up was the burrito bar at Family Esselstyn's house. The choices were replete with flavor, fiber, and deep nutrient richness.

In closing, I made it, I finished. But the truth was WE made it. The WE is Sara and I, she was the core inspiration to set this goal and go after it. There were others quite instrumental in achieving this goal which was set as a rebuilding mark. Continuing to walk away from cancer and walk toward our regular rhythm.

The Temple

Twenty years ago, I was definitely an adult, but I was also able to tap into the innocence and exuberance of childhood. Now, my own childhood is much more distant, and my children and their friends provide the portal I need to remember the roots of my id. When I was twenty, I had a friend with a small sticker on her grungy mountain bike proclaiming, "Your Body is Your Temple," printed in white gothic letters on a black background. Except for an assortment of tattoos, her love of her body was quiet and unassuming – she did not spend much time on hair styles or make-up. Her bodily revelry came through preparing nourishing food and sharing her generous laugh. She was a tremendous athlete – strong, lean, flexible, confident. She played ultimate frisbee, she biked almost everywhere, she was willing to dance most any time and most any place – I have countless pictures of her with her hands up, head tilted, hips one direction and one foot the other. I think of her and I think of that sticker: Your Body is Your Temple. I just love the meaning, the layers, the significance of that concept.

The Bible is often attributed to defining one's body as a holy place. However, I find the direct Biblical quotes to be fairly dark and constricting – 1 Corinthians 6:19 in the English Version Bible reads, "Don't you know that your body is the temple of the Holy Spirit, who lives in you and who was given to you by God?" This verse is immediately after one about "sexual immorality" and before one about how God "bought you for a price." I really can't connect to all of that (and I have a hard time getting excited about a sentence that begins with "Don't you know … ").

What I can connect to is the idea that the fabric of our cells – our beating hearts, our ability to exchange oxygen and carbon dioxide with the plants around us, our dirty fingernails, our shuttling of glucose into hungry mitochondria – all of this is in some way, holy and divine. Whether you are Jewish or Christian or Buddhist or Hindu or Atheist, a temple is a physical space dedicated to worshiping that which you consider sacred. When our body becomes our temple, we transcend religion to celebrate the commonalities of humanity.

The trip to Asheville was a celebration of the connection between our physical bodies and the sacred. Our main reason for going was Greg's participation in the Shut-In Ridge Trail Run. However, even for such a big event, a trip to Asheville brings so much more than a race up a mountain. There is the physical landscape of the Blue Ridge Mountains during autumn. There is the assortment of restaurants serving delicious, farm-to-table food. There is the expected and yet surprising act of meeting friends from Durham. There is the brief yet joyous time we are able to connect with our dear friends from Gainesville, who now live in Asheville.

On the Friday before the race, Greg the kids and my parents went to a pre-race dinner while I went out with a friend. She guided us to a Spanish restaurant with a dish called, berenjenas la taberna, described as "fried eggplant drizzled in wild apiaries honey, garnished with rosemary" (they also snuck in some sea salt). The combination of flavors and textures was as beautiful as it sounds – pure satisfaction of the tongue and the spirit. After dinner we went to a place called The Chocolate Lounge. At this point, I pretty much refuse to go to Asheville unless I'm assured a trip to The Chocolate Lounge. In addition to an assortment of their creamy, rich truffles, I also ordered my "regular" – a warm liquid truffle flavored with honey and lavender.

Over the weekend, we spent time with hometown friends from Gainesville, FL, who moved to Asheville years ago. They live in a cottage on a cozy street, walking distance to downtown. Over the years, we have shared time at the same church, gotten muddy shirts together chasing after Frisbees, and supported each other through pregnancies. In Asheville, we played at the hotel pool and hot tub, cheered Greg at the race finish, shared a "burrito bar" meal together, watched the girls dress up in various costumes, roasted marshmallows out their back deck, and, for the Mamas, stretched in a 90 minute yoga-meditation class.

Greg's race most captures the wisdom of one's body as a temple. It is easier to write about eggplants and honey than about husbands and brain tumors. Perhaps, the profundity is in the facts – Greg had invasive surgery for a malignant brain tumor on July 11th, 2012. He completed numerous blood draws and MRIs and he is taking chemotherapy designed to inhibit rapidly dividing cells, with his most recent pill on October 29th. On the morning of November 3rd, 2012, he ran 19 miles up a mountain on an unpaved trail (the race was supposed to be 18 miles, but part of the Blue Ridge Parkway near the finish was closed and they had to add an extra mile). This was his 9th consecutive, annual running of the race. He made it to the finish with humility and a smile.

Many in Greg's circle never really doubted his ability to run this race, and yet, there is still something miraculous about the triumph of an unbroken spirit over a battered body. With over 7 billion people on the planet today, and countless others who have walked before us, there are stories of weaker humans accomplishing greater feats. On some days, just the simple act of taking a breath is a miracle. I know of people living with chronic pain or physical or mental illness, where waking up and getting out of bed is their triumph of running to the top of the mountain. However, of all of the people out there, and for all of our individual and collective struggles, Greg is the one I stood next to at the altar, he is the one who bathes our children, and he is the one who, after surgery, shook uncontrollably, with two black eyes and his broken head wrapped in gauze.

It is oh so tempting to think of cancer as a betrayal of our corporal home. If your body is your temple, then cancer must be some grave insult to the sacredness of our flesh. Right? I do not believe that cancer is in any way divine. I also do not believe that it is evil or sinister. As I've written before, cancer just is. Those rapidly dividing cells are doing the only thing they know how to do. It is our calling our gift and our burden to try and understand those cells and, when willing and able, to prevent them from consuming our bodies and our spirits.

This year, the Shut-In race finished in the parking lot of the Pisgah Inn. The runners emerged from the woods and then ran down the Blue Ridge Parkway to the finish. The time waiting for Greg was filled with lovely anticipation. Superstorm Sandy left behind piles of snow along the sides of the road. The kids were so very excited at this unexpected find at the top. They threw hard clumps of snow and built as much of a snowman as the small piles in their small hands could muster. As runners came out of the woods, several hundred feet away, we would squint, asking to ourselves and others, "Is that Greg?" No, too tall. No, wrong colored shorts. No, that one's a woman. No, the gait isn't right. Then, finally, he came running down the road. Imagine you could see inside my heart at this moment – fireworks going off, uninhibited dancing, pure jubilation and pride. As he came down the road, the kids ran to meet him. We clapped and cheered and flashed our handmade sign and a collection of flowers. For all of the emotion, our crowd was relatively small and the celebration unassuming. Few, if any, outside of our small group knew of the significance of this momentous occasion.

In so many ways, Greg's finish at Shut-In mirrored his finish at many other events. There was a sense of accomplishment and relief. There were stories of other racers along the trail. There was the gathering of the race shirt and an attempt to start replenishing the body's stores with food and liquid. And yet, this finish was fantastically, tremendously different. Greg's crossing the finish line was holy. It was him saying, "Yes, my body is still my temple." Every step, every breath along those 19 miles was him reminding each of us that through our bodies, we are connected to each other and to that which is sacred.

How Many Fire Throwers Does Your Preschool Have?

Tonight was The Lantern Walk at Abe's (formally Belle's) preschool. This celebration is also called Martinmas Day and is described as, "a time to celebrate our own inner light. It gives many an opportunity to honor that light in preparation for the coming season of winter's darkness."

The evening started indoors, with a sweet play about a lost lamb. The shepherd looks for her lamb as darkness falls. None of the woodland creatures she comes across in the forest know where the lamb has gone. Finally, a gnome with a lantern joins the shepherd girl and together they find and rescue the lamb. Belle was delighted to act out the part of the lamb in the play.

After the play, as darkness fell, each child received a handmade lantern and the whole group – kids and parents – walked along a candlelit path through the school's woodsy backyard. The teachers lead everybody in song, celebrating the candles flickering in the dark. After winding our way through the lit path, we all ended at a bonfire to enjoy baked apples.

Once it was completely dark, the father of one student put on a show involving movement and dance with fire. He had different types of torches that he would spin and swirl and twirl as he danced and moved. The fire made a beautiful whooshing sound as he spun. At one point, he even did an act involving fire breathing!

We thought that this was the grand finale of the evening, but it turns out that the mother of another student knows a type of Indian martial art that also involves twirling fire-lit sticks. She came out and put on another amazing show of fire and dancing in the dark – it was really quite surprising and unexpected. Some kids were more interested in running and swinging freely through the night while everybody else was gathered by the bonfire. But, for the most part, everybody stayed gathered to watch the performances. When the second fire dancer finished her performance, Abe turned to me and said "Mommy, will you go next?" Ha, ha.

Do you know the feeling that comes during a camping trip when everybody is sitting by the fire at the end of the day, watching the flames spark and dance into the night sky? Imagine that energy and feeling, but add people who take sticks of fire that spin and twirl so quickly that the flames blur into arches and circles and swirls. We were entranced.

Whether we are tending to a small candle or to a swirling, spinning torch, I hope that we are all able to tend to our inner lights as we move into the darkness of winter.

Nuts and Bolts

As the fire is aglow in our woodstove and stores are trying to convince me that Christmas season has arrived, spring seems quite far away. Even so, a couple of people have asked about our plans for the Angels Among us 5K on April 20th, 2013. This is a local running event put on by the Duke brain tumor folks to raise money for research. We would like to do a Badousa Brain team this year (Badousa is a moniker Greg and I developed when we were engaged, a combination of my maiden name and his last name). Despite my instincts, we don't need to go into super-planning mode yet.

Today is the blood draw for day 21 of Greg's last cycle of chemo. He was home this morning to help get the kids ready and off to school. He then peddled off to the lab for bloodwork before going into work. Since day 28 of the cycle is on Thanksgiving Day, he'll get the second blood-draw of the cycle on the Monday after Thanksgiving, with the expectation of starting chemo then.

How Not to Cook a Turkey

Today, we head off to the beach for a few days to celebrate Thanksgiving. Belle and I had an unexpected and rewarding adventure after school yesterday. Earlier in the week, I received an e-mail from her school stating that they had for us: "a basket of goodies meant to brighten a challenging year." After getting Belle, we stopped by the office to pick up the basket. The Director of Advancement told me to pull my car around the back of the school to pick up the gift. Hummm … . I needed my car to collect the gift? I pulled around the back of the school to find that the basket was a complete Thanksgiving dinner with boxes and boxes of canned items, pasta, sauce, cake mix, plus perishables including a turkey, milk, and eggs. It was enough to feed about 20 people for a Thanksgiving dinner or a family of 4 for a few days. I was very surprised and did my best to show appropriate gratitude.

Because we were heading off to the beach for a week, we couldn't make use of the generosity. My gut told me to share this bounty with a family in need. Through work, I knew of a family with limited resources and many mouths to feed. Earlier in the week, this mother asked if I knew of any charities in the area that provided meals for Thanksgiving. After asking around, the only resource I learned of was a wait list at the Department of Social Services. I called Greg and explained the situation and he agreed that it made sense to share our gift. I happened to have the phone number for the mother of this family in my work cell phone (it is the only patient number I have programmed in my phone). I knew that she and her children had just moved because she couldn't afford the rent and utilities at her previous home. I didn't have her new address. She answered when I called. I explained the situation and she said that she would be grateful to receive the food. On Thursday, our family and theirs will be blessed with tables of good food and full bellies.

So far, the beach has blessed us with comfortable temperatures and blue skies. The only bump was when my Dad looked at the oven at 3pm and realized that it was off. My Mom had put the turkey in to bake around 1pm and somehow the oven got turned off, but we had no idea when. We fired the oven back up again and made plans to eat a couple of hours later than planned.

We brought our four bikes to the beach and Greg has gone out for an early morning ride each day. He and I went for a run yesterday and I got in a run today. The kids did a little biking yesterday, and I'm sure we'll all be out on our bikes again tomorrow. The beach is relatively sleepy over Thanksgiving, and we can bike the grid between the ocean and the intercoastal waterway with little fear of frustrated drivers.

Even with the oven misfortune, Thanksgiving dinner came together. We sat down together by around 6pm to feast on our day's labors. Our meal's blessing came from something the kids learned at The Children's Garden:

For the golden corn and the apples on the trees
For the golden butter and the honey from the bees
For fruits and nuts and berries we gather on the way
We thank you for the food we eat, we thank you every day
Blessings on our meal

Back to Life

I awoke this morning with the lyrics from the Soul 2 Soul song "Back to Life" in my head:

Back to life, back to reality
Back to life, back to reality
Back to the here and now, yeah

These words drifted through my brain after a 1am wake-up from poor Abe when he wet his bed, soaking his top sheets and comforter. Then, at 4a, we heard him yell "Mommy!!! My door is O-PEN." Apparently, we'd neglected to shut it after the 1am shenanigans. Then, there's the "beep, beeeep, beeeeeeep" of my alarm at 5:30a. In-between all of this, my brain decided to worry about Christmas and work and my lack of food prep for the week and my dental work next week. Ahhhh, back to life.

So, we rolled out of bed and started the day. I managed to scrape together all of our lunches (thank you to Target for their post-Halloween Z-bar sale). The kids and I made it out the door by 7:25a, ready to tackle the day.

Greg loaded up the bike trailer with his work items for the week and biked off to the laboratory for his end-of-chemo-cycle bloodwork – then to work. It amazes me each and every time I see him bike off to the lab on a Monday morning – loaded down with all of his belongings. He never complains about the ride. He sees it as a practical way to meet his clinical and transportation needs, as a way to sneak in some exercise, and as a way to reduce his carbon footprint. In some sense, this unfolding miracle has now become a regular part of his routine.

We expect Greg will start cycle four of chemo in the next day or so. The oncology RN says that he is a "late nadirer" in that his blood counts, mainly his platelets, drop to their low point late in the cycle. Once we get the go-ahead, then I'll pick up the chemo and he'll start the next round.

Have a Blessed Day

A common way to say good-bye is "Have a nice day" or maybe "I hope you have a nice/good day." Over the past few years, I've noticed that quite a few of my patients say, "Have a blessed day." I'm guessing that this is a Southern thing, but I'm not sure. Some patients say it to me in person and others have it as part of their voice mail greeting.

A few weeks ago, as I was leaving somebody's house, I said with a smile, "You have a blessed day." I'd never said these words before in this context and I hadn't planned on saying it, it just came out without conscious thought. I perceived that this person gave me a funny look, but maybe this was really my own brain going, "Huh? You've never said that before!" When I had trouble reaching this person after a couple of phone calls, paranoia kicked in. I worried that perhaps there was a cultural or racial aspect to saying "Have a blessed day" that I missed out on and that I'd accidentally offended the person.

I considered asking a coworker if I'd stepped in it without meaning to, but my paranoia was enough that I didn't want to risk further embarrassment. I searched Google, and found the following:

http://www.msatheists.org/2012/06/have-blessed-day-challenge.html

> *"Now, if the have-a-nice-day thing was mildly irritating to me, the have-a-blessed-day thing is like nails on the chalkboard because it is so damned presumptuous, unnecessary, and it inserts god-belief, one might even say proselytizing, into that two second interaction at the gas station. The clerk is making a declaration of god-belief (evangelical, personal-Jesus god-belief, no less), and she is presuming that I share in that personal god-belief, making a neutral transaction all-of-the-sudden political. It irritates me so much that I go out of my way to avoid the clerks who I know to be Blessed-Day wishers."*

Wow, that person is pretty pissed.

Even though I generally don't say "Have a blessed day" (and perhaps I won't again), when I hear it from another person, it strikes me as a tender way to part. Perhaps naively, I never assumed any pretense of religion or God in the saying. I figured that while the speaker of "Have a blessed day" likely believes in God, the recipient can receive the farewell in simple kindness.

The definition of "blessed*" is flexible regarding the presence of God. I have no idea if I offended the person to whom I was speaking and am saddened that a tenderhearted phrase upon departure can make somebody angry. I've wondered if there are other gentle ways to say farewell that go beyond "Have a nice day" but carry less religious weight than "Have a blessed day." One could say, "Have a graceful day" but that might result in a funny look. One could say "Have a groovy day" but Birkenstocks and braids might be required for that one. "Namaste" only works at the yoga studio or in the Whole Foods aromatherapy aisle. "Hasta luego" can work, but has the potential to be dicey among strangers.

I'll most likely stick with "Have a nice day" for now. I'll also hope that as we go out into the world and interact with friends and neighbors and strangers, that we will assume the best in others and that we will be open to the best in ourselves.

*http://www.merriam-webster.com/dictionary/blessed

Definition of BLESSED
1a: held in reverence b : honored in worship c : beatific
2: of or enjoying happiness; specifically: enjoying the bliss of heaven
3: bringing pleasure, contentment, or good fortune

Papi Turns 60-something-or-other-plus-or-minus

Last night we celebrated my Dad's, aka "Papi's", birthday at my folk's house. He turned 60-something-or-other-plus-or-minus. My day was super hectic and included fun things like chopping pineapple, baking squash, making granola, putting a car seat in the attic, cleaning the downstairs, trying to organize the clutter in Belle's room, and shuttling kids to and from school. Earlier in the week, Greg and I talked about biking over to my folks' house for the birthday celebration – they live less than 2 miles from us along safe, neighborhood roads. Greg and I knew the general plan for the evening, but we didn't coordinate the details. Around 5p, I left a message for Greg at work. At 5:15p, I went ahead and got our bikes out and hooked up. Belle rides on a tag-a-long, a child's bike that attaches to an adult bike. Abe rides in the Chariot, a little pod that attaches to the other adult bike (it's what Greg uses to bring stuff into work). At 5:30p Belle, Abe, and I were all set and ready to go, but no Greg. Grrrrr. The kids were running around the yard and I was trying hard to not be annoyed (or worried). Around 5:45p, Abe buckled himself into the Chariot. Both kids were chanting "Where's Daddy?? Where's Daddy?" A couple of minutes later, Greg arrived home.

I knew that I shouldn't be upset, that Greg didn't know the schedule that I'd mapped out during the day (Alas, his super-hero powers do not include mind reading). I was flustered that we were running late and Greg was flustered at coming home to a family that was packed up and antsy to go. Still, he put his work stuff down and was ready to head off on the bikes in a very timely manner. We peddled off into the evening.

We ended up having a lovely dinner with my parents, Noah, and Yvonne. Birthdays are a time to show appreciation and gratitude for those we love. There really is nothing that we can give or say to my Dad to fully express how we feel. He and my Mom have always been defined by a wonderful combination of wisdom and generosity. Since Greg's surgery, my Dad has helped us in so many ways – caring for Belle and Abe, providing transportation, taking photographs, listening to worries, attending school events, contributing financially, and sharing laughs. He generally does not like to be the center of attention. During this evening, it was nice to take the time to celebrate him. His gifts included a mix of books, music, and clothes. Abe picked out a monster truck for him.

Here's the conversation at the store:

Me: *Abe, what do you want to get Papi for his birthday?*

Abe: *A monster truck!*

Me: *Are you sure Papi wants a monster truck?*

Abe: *Yes! Yes he does! A big monster truck that goes vvvvrrrroooommmmm.*

Me: *OK, then let's get him a monster truck.*

Miraculously, the monster truck peacefully stayed at my parents' house when we left. I was certain that Abe would melt down when he realized that the truck really was for Papi and not him. Belle got Papi some playing cards, a bag of polished rocks, and a small box of snowman "Peeps." Both kids were very excited for him to open the gifts they'd selected. I was happy that I'd decided not to steer them towards more practical gifts. It was sweet to have them share gifts that they picked out themselves.

Another neat aspect of the gifts my Dad received was that each giver included some type of art. My Mom painted a beautiful card on handmade paper – a tangled tree filled with bright leaves and birds. Noah and Yvonne wrote a poem in his card. Belle and Abe's gifts were each wrapped in pictures they'd drawn. Greg and I gave him a collage card. We are generally a bunch of nerdy academics (or engineers), so it was fun to see the different expressions of our creative sides. It is lovely that Papi inspires poetry and art from the people who love him.

After presents and cake, we bundled up to peddle back home. The night was cold and crisp, with the low expected to drop into the 30s. Greg and I were most definitely worn out from the week, but Belle and Abe were glowing on the bike ride home (and revved up on sugar-infused lemon cake). Belle said several times, "Mommy, is it past my bedtime? I am not tired at all!" They each had heart-filled smiles and an awareness of the unusual journey of being out on bikes for a nighttime ride. The neighborhood was aglow with holiday decorations and lights. Some houses had simple candle lights in each window and others had every bush and tree adorned with multitudes of lights in bright colors. Even though I was a bit flustered at the beginning of the night, seeing

Belle and Abe soaking in the love and the lights reminded me that every moment is just that – a moment. With patience, the frustrations of a long day were replaced by our family bundled up and peddling home through the chilly night, taking in the darkness and the stars and the bright holiday lights.

Christmas Angels

Last Thursday, I went out to dinner with a group of women to celebrate the upcoming marriage of a friend. We enjoyed Asian cuisine seated around a low, rectangular table in a back room, set aside just for us. I arrived late, and as I was sitting down, I heard a friend I hadn't seen in a while say, "I'm sorry … ." She was interrupted and didn't finish her sentence. As I found a spot at the table and processed her words, my first thought was, "What could she be sorry about?" I sat down next to her and she finished her sentence, "I'm sorry to hear about Greg." We talked for a bit and I let her know that Greg is healing, recovered from surgery, and tolerating chemo fairly well. I realized that this may have been the first time I didn't immediately register somebody's reference to Greg's cancer. I took my being stumped at her initial, unfinished comment as a good sign – as a sign that my mental space is more filled with Greg's health and vibrancy than with his cancer.

Things changed after this moment of mental space. Somehow, the rest of the weekend ended up being filled with reminders of all that Greg has been through in the past 6 months. On Saturday morning, out-of-town friends came over for breakfast. As he talked to our friends about his cancer journey, I realized how long it had been since he'd fully told his story. In hearing Greg describe the past few months, I sensed him taking a new ownership of all that has happened to him.

Over the past couple of weeks, Greg has been an informal advocate for another local brain tumor patient. He has talked with this person and shared his experiences – of diagnosis through surgery and back into day-to-day life. This person had surgery over the past few days. We've had access to the website set up to share news about those scary days surrounding surgery. It was strange for Greg and me to see photographs from another patient before and after surgery. Prior to surgery, doctors strategically place sticky-pads with small, greenish, marble-looking orbs on them onto the patient's head. These orbs help guide the precision of the pre-surgical MRI and the actual surgery. Greg and I vividly remember his night before surgery, with his head decorated with strange pads that look like something out of a science fiction movie – a way for extraterrestrial beings to communicate directly with our inner thoughts. These orbs represented both the seriousness of the procedure and the extent of the medical technology available to help make sure that all goes as planned. Greg said it was unsettling for him to read the comments other people posted during and after this person's surgery, knowing that his own friends and family went through similar emotions with his surgery.

One of the most powerful moments of the Christmas story is when the angel appears to Mary and says to her, "Fear not, Mary. God has been gracious to you." How many times in our lives do we need an angel to come to us and say, "Fear not."? Over the past couple of weeks, I have sensed that I have been visited by angels with messages of comfort. The first one came to me as I was enjoying an evening with friends around a dinner table. Her message was "Be free – you have the ability to put your worries aside and celebrate the joy of friendship." The second angel came to me as Greg shared his cancer story with friends. She said "Your husband has an amazing story. He owns this story and will weave it into something of beauty." The third angel came as Greg helped somebody facing the darkness of a brain mass. This angel said, "Your greatest gift is to transform your pain into blanket and to use that blanket to provide warmth and strength and comfort to others in need." This season, I am grateful for the messages of angels.

Broken Hearts

This Christmas was about broken hearts. My heart broke when a gunman shot his way into a school and killed twenty-six children and teachers. My heart broke when somebody I love chose not to extend a holiday dinner invitation to a friend because of a political bumper sticker on a car. My heart broke when people I love could not share in the beauty of a candlelight Christmas service because that church welcomes everybody, including same sex couples, to the communion table. Can a lesbian pastor give communion? Oh yes she can! She brought God into our home when she visited Greg after his first surgery, sitting with him in stillness and silence, offering a simple prayer before leaving. Without her voice and her presence, God would be much, much further away. My heart broke when I tried to help a patient whose child was taken away because of broken bones. My heart broke when I looked at the bounty given to my family this holiday season and I thought of those with less to celebrate.

And yet, every time my heart broke over the past few weeks, Grace stepped in and said "mend." Grace said, "Be patient, be loving, be strong, be forgiving. Your heart is still beating. You still have love. Carry on and do not give up your desire for a better world." Every time my heart broke this Christmas season, something burst in and shouted "NO!!" There were many times when Greg said something that made me laugh (he is so very good at making me laugh). There were times when I made myself laugh (like when the best I could come up with on Christmas Eve was "Merry F-ing Christmas.") On the winter solstice, a group of families gathered in the darkness to participate in a Spiral Walk – an evening of greenery and seashells and children and candles and a gentle cello made to sing by the hands of a child.

After a brain tumor, after surgery, and during chemotherapy, my husband was by my side each and every moment this holiday season. He was by my side for three church services. He was by my side for the assembly of a multitude of electronic toys. He charged more batteries than humanly possible. Even when I was left by others whom I love, Greg stood by me for every single moment of this amazing holiday season. On Christmas Eve, when my heart was broken with the loneliness of being left by people I love, our family visited dear friends who welcomed us with open arms and smiles and wine.

Earlier this week, I participated in an advent parenting group at church. We reflected on the year and on the light that comes from stars and candles and spirits. The pastor leading the group asked us to bring something that represented Joy. I brought a cookbook. I love cooking for people I care about. I love taking bare essentials and using knives and heat to bring bounty to our wooden table. During this group, we shared in a prayer that captures this holiday season.

O Christ/Love, how shall we meet you, how welcome you aright?
Find space
Name joy
Rise up
Share love

O Christ/Love, how shall we know you, recognize you in the shadows?
Look inward
Expect surprise
Reach out
Listen closely

Yo Buddy, Can I Get a Ride?

We are now a one car family. If you'd asked me a year ago whether we could get by with one car, I would have said, "We would if we had to, but it would be really difficult, and we'd have to give up some things." Greg's willingness and ability to bike, share rides with friends, and take the bus has made having one car a non-issue. With Greg's parents in town for Christmas, I thought that our one-car-ness would be put to the test. Fortunately, it has gone quite smoothly.

Over this week, we have borrowed cars from two sets of friends and from my parents. This enabled the six of us to get to multiple activities together. We only imposed on people twice. We've been able to get to the movies, to church, and to a family ice skating adventure. Everybody we borrowed a vehicle from was more than willing and gracious to lend us their wheels for a few hours. It was nice to be able to count on our circle to help us out.

Tomorrow is Greg's full day at the cancer center – bloodwork, MRI, and meeting with the oncologist. He will likely start round 5 of chemo in the next day or so.

In Greg's Words

Love for Sara

I have wondered about lots of things, naturally before a brain tumor as well. But since the brain tumor I wonder more about the immediate loved ones, in this case Sara.

My world was narrow, harrowingly. In the near period of a seizure and being told I had a 2-inch diameter mass in my skull a lot of other things went quiet. I found myself in a corner and it is where I do not want to be.

My first indication of an abnormality occurred 9 hours away by car from my wife. When my senses returned to me in the ER in Montgomery, AL I could not speak to my wife. I had to tell a friend what I wanted said to her before I tried to speak to her on the telephone. That way when I immediately choked up and could not speak he could take the phone and convey the necessary information. After he left the ER one of the nurses gave me her phone (and charger) cord so I could call her again. Sara's voice never wavered, mine was crumbling, she conveyed a steadfast grounding in this initial frightening period.

Down the road a few days and weeks it was all Sara. She led appointments, tracking calls/emails, researching the loose ends we could not yet figure out, and counseling me. I did not worry. I was in a corner, I fight, Sara was in the corner with me. Further with Sara being a nurse and having a longstanding relationship with my new primary care physician my care just fell into place and I was operating on trust. In a sense my road has been easy and narrow.

I wonder frequently about Sara's road. I think the caregiver of one stricken has a harder path. Not only do they have to be utterly shocked by an event like a grand mal occurring far away, they must also consider too many what-ifs, one of which involves an event we are all guaranteed of by virtue of birth. Oh, and then she has to handle all the driving, the kids, groceries, food prep, laundry, and on and on and on; numbing.

In this holiday season, as before it, I salute my wife. I can't imagine the role she has had to bear and for the early portion of it, she could not vent to me. Remember for a while I was happy just to watch the paint dry on the wall, paint that was put there 6 years ago.

I did not learn anything new about appreciation of life or shortness of life from my brain tumor. I have cemented further the gratitude and depth of love for my wife.

Cycle Five

The flow at the cancer center has become familiar – bloodwork, MRI, meeting with mid-level practitioner who does neuro checks, and meeting with oncologist who reviews the bloodwork and images. Last stop is always at the pharmacy. One order of chemo, coming up. Greg was seen by a new mid-level practitioner this time. She did the usual neuro checks and then sat to answer questions. She mentioned that Greg's bloodwork and MRI looked good, but we would discuss these with the neuro-oncologist. In addition to the labs and MRI, Greg also brought up a race opportunity called Kona Inspired and the possibility of driving.

After a childhood of hockey and BMX, Greg's current sport of choice is the triathlon. The Stanley Cup of triathlons is the Ironman World Championships in Kona Hawaii – a 2.4 mile swim and 112 mile bike, with a marathon to finish. To qualify, an athlete must place in the top one or two finishers in their age group in a qualifying event. While Greg is a strong, competent athlete, he likely wouldn't quality for this event competing in the open market. Last year, Kona started a contest called "Kona Inspired" where people with athletic talent and an inspiring story enter to win spot in the race. Athletes submit a 90-second video sharing their story. The videos are posted online where people can vote.

Greg is considering submitting a video for Kona 2013. We hoped to get a few shots of Greg during this visit to the cancer center, to include in the video. We learned that it is not possible to video the MRI, because the magnet is powerful and always turned on. When we met with the oncologist, she requested that we talk to a social worker in the center, to get her input on taking pictures and video. We ended up not getting any photos or video, but we got the sense that we may be able to come back sometime soon to get the images we wanted.

We also asked about the timeline for Greg to start driving again and were surprised to learn that he may be able to start driving in the next month or so (six months after his initial seizure). Greg's driving seems to have been somewhat of a moving target, where we never got a consistent answer or path to his getting behind the wheel again. This time, the provider said that Greg could take a voluntary, computerized driving assessment to gauge his driving skills and abilities. This test isn't legally required, but gives input on the skills needed for driving. Somewhat confusingly, the oncologist can give him a green light to drive without this computerized test.

We've tried to better understand Greg's seizure risk – mainly for driving, swimming, and other potentially dangerous activities. The RN for the oncologist seems to be the most concerned and the neurosurgeon seems to be the least concerned. The RN says, "Never, ever go up into the attic without somebody else home." The surgeon says, "So long as you're not driving or swimming, what's the worst that could happen? You may fall and flop around a bit, but you should be fine. I've never had a patient have a seizure while driving." Because he had one seizure, because he had a brain tumor, and because his brain sustained some level of trauma from surgery, he is at an increased risk of seizure. Because he only had one seizure, because surgery was successful in removing most of the tumor, and because he is on seizure control medicine, his risk is low. The question is how to balance living a full life with a low seizure risk.

Another fuzzy area of Greg's brain tumor puzzle is his prognosis. There are less aggressive tumors than what Greg had, but there are also more aggressive tumors. One of his oncologists said that brain tumors are more like fruit cake than a block of cheddar cheese – the tumor is a mix of all different types of cells, not a collection of one cell type. If a pathologist finds any cells that are more aggressive, then the whole tumor gets classified as the more aggressive type. During this most recent meeting with the oncologist, the oncologist said that for patients with more aggressive tumors, 10 to 15% of the tumor cells are fast growing. For Greg's tumor, only 3% of the tumor was fast growing. This is good.

Greg's MRI shows that the surgical site is healing. It also shows what the oncologist calls "post-surgical changes." We're not completely sure what this means, but we think it just means changes in the tissue from surgery, as opposed to cancer. There is still some tumor that can be seen on the images, but the MRI images with contrast do not show any of the aggressive, fast-growing cells. We left the meeting with the oncologist thinking that the surgical site is healing well and that there are no detectible cancer cells left. The oncologist also said that if the MRI ever detects the fast-growing cancer cells, then Greg would do radiation and a different type of chemotherapy. With frequent and regular MRIs, any new cancer that could show up would be detected and treated quickly.

When Greg and I talk about and process all that the oncologist says, we really don't like hearing how well prepared they are for the possibility of new cancer appearing. We'd much rather they talk with certainty about a path that includes no more cancer. However, we've known from the beginning that Greg will be monitored for the rest of his life.

The oncologist was pleased with Greg's bloodwork and gave the OK for him to start the next cycle of chemo right away. We headed down to the pharmacy and were happy to see our usual pharmacist, exchanging New Year's greetings. There frequently seems to be some hang-up in picking up Greg's chemo at the end of the day. This time, the MD had forgotten to sign the order. We got this straightened out and left the cancer center with chemo in-hand.

Roots

Belle and Abe definitely hit the jackpot in the Grandparent lottery. They have three sets of grandparents – one set here in Durham, one in Montana, and one in Rhode Island. All of the grandparents bring different experiences and personalities into Belle and Abe's lives, along with lots and lots of love. A year or so ago, we developed a set of family rules which we wrote in bright crayon on a large sheet of paper in the kitchen. They include the usual stuff like, "No hitting or yelling," plus some fun stuff like, "Wipe boogies on a tissue." A few months after the house rules went up, I realized that we also needed to post some consequences. The consequences include time-out, no treat, and no friends/computer time. The last consequence, to be used when all else fails, is, "Ask grandparents for input." I would be completely comfortable calling any of the six grandparents for this "last resort" consequence. I know that each one would help us approach the situation with compassion and wisdom and opportunity for learning and growth.

Greg's parents flew down from Rhode Island to spend Christmas with us here in Durham. In the past, we haven't had a proper guest room. We use a room downstairs that is a combined study/guest room, but it doesn't have a door. This room is at the bottom of our stairs, between the kitchen and the front door. When guests come, we hang a blanket in the open space to create some sense of privacy. While Greg's parents have always been gracious about this set-up, I wanted to make a space more welcoming for company. Before they came, we reorganized some furniture so that Abe's room became a temporary guest room. Unlike his sister, who collects everything on the planet, Abe's room is not littered with toys and remnants of nature (rocks, acorns, feathers, pinecones, shells, etc). For this visit, Greg's parents stayed in the new guest room, with a proper door, away from the fray of the downstairs hustle and bustle. Abe slept with us for the week, which gave us the added benefit of a sweet, snugly little boy in our bed.

Greg's parents have been very supportive of us over the past year. In the week before surgery, Belle and Abe flew up to spend a week in RI without us, while Greg and I stayed in Durham. With the stress of surgery and the newness of a big trip without Mom and Dad, Belle and Abe were nurtured and loved during this week. Their time in RI included the magic of summertime in New England – picnics and swimming and playtime with relatives and holiday parades. They even adopted a wayward duck! With the geographic distance, Greg's parents stayed connected to us through phone calls and e-mails and letters.

Christmas was their first visit to us since the summer. Our house is a hectic place to visit, with four busy, active folks always playing, cooking, working, e-mailing, and even dancing at times. When they visit, Greg's parents slide right into the mix and join in the chaos and the fun. For this visit, as in all visits in the past, Greg's Mom, Grami, whipped up a batch of Portuguese soup to nourish us during the week. She brought toys, games, and crafts for the kids. She made peppermint bark with Belle and spend time playing multiple rounds of mancala with her. Greg's Dad, Grampy, brought his gifts and talents as well. Much to my delight, he assigns himself as the official dish washer after meals (how lucky can a daughter-in-law be??). He made an effort to get the kids outside and he wasn't squeamish about their running, jumping, biking, and playing in the dirt. If the weather was bad, he brought the kids in for rounds of tic-tac-toe or matchbox car races. We have an open-door policy with friends and neighbors on our street, and Greg's parents welcomed the assortment of people who stopped by unexpectedly.

Thanks to Grami and Grampy's stellar kid wrangling skills, Greg and I even got some alone time during Christmas week. One evening, we went to Only Burger and to the movies to see Skyfall. It is so nice to sit down to a meal with Greg and to relax and talk without distractions. Greg's parents also kept the kids on the day we went to the cancer center and again the next day, when we both had to work.

Christmas morning was a bonanza of toys and books and clothes and chocolate. Greg's parents were generous, and the kids awoke to a storybook morning of bursting stockings and an abundance of new playthings. We wove in a breakfast of baked goods, bacon, and eggs and spent the day playing, cooking, listening to music, and enjoying the warmth of family.

Greg's parents bring support, generosity, patience, and love to our family. They helped bring Greg into his world. While he is a unique individual, he is also a reflection of their genes, their love, their talents, their ability to nurture, their thoughtfulness, their wisdom, and their strength. As our family continues to face and challenges and joys in the year ahead, we do so with the foundation of grandparents, near and far.

Buckets

I've heard of the "bucket analogy" to describe some allergies. The thought is that people have a hypothetical bucket that reflects their tolerance to allergens. Our immune system is equipped to manage exposure to a certain amount of whatever we may be allergic to. Exposure to allergens adds to the bucket. If the bucket is only partially full, then the person doesn't have symptoms – their body is managing the exposure. However, if the bucket gets full, then exposure to allergens, even a small amount, causes to bucket to overfill and allergy symptoms kick in. The trick to avoid all of the sneezing and mucus is to keep the bucket from overfilling. This can be done by reducing exposure (which keeps the bucket from filling) and/or taking medications (which makes the bucket bigger).

The other day, I started thinking about the bucket analogy for anger. It takes very little to piss me off these days. I quickly get stewing over just about anything: lost keys, speeding drivers, diabetic patients who don't take their insulin, Belle and Abe giving me grief over brushing their teeth before bed for the 4th night in a row, our cluttered living room, the pile of unread books by my bed, stubbing my toe on the door jam, making lunches at 10pm when I really need to be in bed, and so on. My anger bucket is full, full, full. Belle asks me to help find a lost toy for the 5th time in 2 minutes and I'm boiling. I envision going into her room and taking armloads of her toys and dumping them in the trash. In reality, I still manage to muster the patience to tell her to find another toy to play with and I'll help her look once I'm done with the dishes.

I am angry over the trials and tribulations that come with Greg's cancer. I am angry at the day-to-day worry (What if he gets the flu? What if he falls off his bike?). I get angry at the long-term worry (What if the cancer returns? What if he develops a serious reaction to his medicine?). I'm angry when I don't understand the oncologist. I'm angry when the lab doesn't have the order for his bloodwork, and he has to wait an extra 45 minutes. I'm angry when time, energy, and money are spent at medical appointments instead of cooking, running, or playing with the kids.

I need to keep my anger bucket less full, else I might explode. If I could empty the bucket, then when a driver zooms by me at 65 MPH in a 45 MPH zone, I could take a breath and let it go, instead of clenching my teeth, getting a pit in my stomach, and thinking nasty thoughts. I read an article suggesting that one way to reduce anger is cultivate patience – but how the heck am I supposed to be patient when I have 42 things to do and 2 hours to do them in? I don't have the answer. I know that there are some things I can do to help empty my bucket – grabbing an early morning run, nibbling on a glossy bar of dark chocolate, talking with a friend, writing, sliding into my smooth sheets before 10p, talking and breathing with God, being present during church. Still, I haven't figured out how to empty my anger bucket and keep it from filling again too quickly. Some days I just think, "Fuck it, I'll just be angry."

Belle's class has a bucket filling activity. The teacher hung a picture of a big bucket on a wall in the class. When a student does something good, then the teacher tapes a construction paper rain drop to the bucket. The kids can do things like look for a lost item, help a friend with a difficult task, clean up after an activity, or show an unexpected act of kindness. When the bucket is filled with drops, then the class gets to do a fun activity, like watch a movie or bring a stuffed animal or small toy to class the next day. I like the idea of a bucket of kindness and goodness, where the goal is to fill it until it spills over and then fill it again. Instead of spilling resulting in sneezing or frustration, it results in good things spilling out into the world.

I haven't figured out my anger bucket. Somewhat ironically, at this exact moment, I am trying to finish writing; Greg is moving firewood from the trailer to the back yard; Abe is sliding back and forth on the rowing machine behind me; and Belle is scrunched up in this chair next to me, wriggling around, trying to type on the keyboard and threatening to cut my hair. I promised Abe that I would write for 5 more minutes and then help him build another Lego car. Hopefully, he'll remember to put the Legos back in the Lego bucket when he's done…

In Greg's Words

Days, Months, Years

Things can happen in a matter of days, or at least show themselves after having been there for a long time. On June 17, 2012 I was given a free ticket by the family. Equipped with reflective gear and many lights I set out on my bike before dawn. I also had a bag on my back which contained my swim gear. It was Father's day and I was making the beautiful journey about 25 miles south to New Hope Landing on Jordan Lake. I did not spend much time biking in the dark that morning because of the time of year. That time of the day is my time to exercise, my time to just be, the world slowly waking up and very few cars. Many mornings in Belle's first and second year of life I would put her in my lap, pull the rocking chair to the open window, and tell her we are watching the world go by. That consisted of trees, squirrels, birds, clouds, a rising sun, and the feeling of the morning air. I arrived at the lake and chained my bike up. I put on my swim clothes and waited for the 1 mile swim to begin. I had not been swimming much so I started near the end and went very slow. I recall vividly that as I neared the finish there were docks protruding in the water. And on one of the docks I saw my family, I lifted my head to let them know I saw them. What a fantastic day. Again, that was June 17, the mass in my head was there and lying-in-wait. 4 days later I seized and another chapter began.

Things can happen in a matter of months. On July 11, 2012 I was doped up and knocked out so that modern medicine could work on cleaning me up and giving me normal longevity. What a trip, still unfolding. Today I went to the pool for exercise, swimming laps. I went yesterday too. I have long loved athletics for many reasons which includes the feeling of plying effort and then getting an improvement in return. I am far from plying consistency right now. However, I had 2 days in a row and a guy has to have fantasies. Today's set was 4 x 200 on 3:45. I did the first 3 on 3:15. I opened up a little for the fourth one for a few reasons. I realized it may have been near a year since the last time I taxed myself in the pool with hard swimming, where your lungs feel like they are about to burst but you can't give in yet as there is still 75 yards to go, so you must find peace and bring that to meet chosen stress. Also, I wanted to see if I could sneak under 3 minutes. 6 months later on January 11, 2013 I snuck under 3:00 for my fourth 200 SCY repeat.

I look forward to life's magic unfolding as the years proceed.

Happy New Year

Belle's class wrote their New Year's Resolutions and posted them outside of the classroom. Belle's said, "My goal this year is to help uthrs." It was fun to read what the kids wrote. Belle's was relatively simple, while others were more detailed (and involved things like reading more and doing their homework). I chuckled at one of her classmates who wrote, "My goal this year is to finish first grade." Then, I remembered that her younger brother died last year from a blood cancer. Suddenly, her goal seemed much more noble and poignant.

I am excited for the year ahead. I am excited for blessings that reveal themselves each day. I am excited for the birthdays and holidays and family vacations. I am excited for Greg to finish chemo. Looking forward in anticipation feels antithetical to the mantra of "living in the moment." If we spend too much time thinking into the future, imagining future sunsets and bike rides and birthday cakes, then we may somehow dilute the pleasures right at our fingertips this very moment. Still, sometimes my imagination takes over, creeping into the future. I take a moment to look beyond brain tumors and deceased friends and relatives and continued news of violence and prejudice and know that the possibility of joy is waiting for us just around the corner.

Drivin' Ms. Crazy

It is a busy week. Greg took a driving test at the cancer center on Monday that didn't involve any actual driving. I only heard a brief explanation, but it sounded like the test involved measures of his reaction time, peripheral vision, and how well he perceives color. He was supposed to hear back by the end of the day today, but no word yet. He feels like it went fine.

Tomorrow is his first blood draw of Cycle Five of chemo. He'll bike to the lab in the morning and then head into work.

T.G.F.I.

Thank Goodness for Insurance

We spent the afternoon at the Duke ED after Abe flipped off his bike and hit his face on a rock. He split his cheek open and the cut went through to the inside of his mouth (which we couldn't tell, at first). I took him to the Urgent Care down the street, and they pretty quickly sent us to the ED. We went home after a round of pain-relieving, amnesia-inducing medicine and about 9 stitches. On the drive home, his eyes were heavy and tired, the side of his face swollen and drooping like a stroke patient, a sad sight to see. Abe will feast on ice cream and smoothies for a while.

Stream of Consciousness

Greg rides his bike to the lab for this bloodwork this morning. It is 28 degrees F. He wears many layers. When he gets home in the evening, he tells me about a driver who tried to run him off the road to get to the turn lane for the interstate. He has stories like this almost every day.

Abe's face is healing. He is my broken boy. He eats and drinks from the right side of his mouth.

I sit in a training to learn software we use to chart patient encounters. The room is small and crowded. Everybody has a laptop, as instructed. Using this charting system, my future self will chart that Mrs. Cabel takes 25mg of metoprolol instead of 50mg. She lost track of the prescription given to her at the hospital and is still taking her old dose. She has heart failure, diabetes, hypertension, gout, hyperlipidemia, and asthma. I will chart that Mr. Pell, who weighs 517 pounds, wants to lose weight – he says that this is his primary health concern. He has weighed over 500 pounds for 8 years. Ideally, he would like to weigh in the mid-300s, like he did when his children were born. He wants gastric by-pass surgery, but he weighs too much. He says he'll go south of the border for surgery, if he has to. I will chart that when I visit Mr. Blanch at home, who was denied coverage for a skilled nursing facility after his last hospitalization, he cannot cook, clean, do laundry, get to the bathroom in time, or walk down his back steps. He is stubborn and refuses to use his walker. The right lens on his glasses is cracked beyond repair. His house is a mess. It stinks. His feet are swollen and purple. His face lights up when he describes the doctor from his first heart surgery as a child.

I get distracted during the training, my mind wanders. There is my laptop. I read a post by Tim Kreider about the consequences of removing the sick and elderly from sight – tucked away in hospitals and nursing homes. He writes, "Segregating the old and the sick enables a fantasy, as baseless as the fantasy of capitalism's endless expansion, of youth and health as eternal, in which old age can seem to be an inexplicably bad lifestyle choice, like eating junk food or buying a minivan, that you can avoid if you're well-educated or hip enough. So that when through absolutely no fault of your own your eyesight begins to blur and you can no longer eat whatever you want without consequence and the hangovers start lasting for days, you feel somehow ripped off, lied to." He writes this at the end of his article, "life is not a story or an adventure or a journey of spiritual self-discovery; it's a slog. And it orders us to keep going, don't you dare give up, no matter what" (New York Times, January 20, 2013).

I drift from this article to one about running form. The jury is still out about whether people are meant to first strike their heel or their midfoot or their forefoot when running. Fifty percent of runners report some type of injury each year. My hamstring is sore. I have not run since December.

The training ends and I head to the city pool. The pool is closed for public swim until 8p. I call Greg. I pick him up from work. We stop on the way home and collect three oak rounds left behind under the power lines. Greg estimates that if this wood were split and put up for sale in front of the grocery store, it would be worth over $30. Tonight, we are going to our first concert in over ten years. We are using a new babysitter.

My parents bring the kids home. Their bellies are full. Belle has read for 20 minutes and practiced her spelling words. The bonus word this week is "science." We get the kids ready for bed and the babysitter arrives. She has bright eyes and a smile fueled by good energy. We are comfortable leaving her to guard the fort.

On the way to Carrboro, we hit an unexpected traffic jam. We crawl, 5 MPH, red taillights snake in front of us. I say that it must be a big accident or a UNC basketball game. Turns out to be both. Greg is driving. After a 20-minute wait, a police officer directs us around a mangled car. There is a circle of flares along the road. The occupants' lives changed in a second. We don't know their story.

Yo La Tengo. One of Greg's favorite bands. We park a couple of blocks away and walk through the chilly night to get to the venue. We cross the street twice to get around construction. We walk by Carrburritos. This restaurant always makes me think of my sister, Kim. I have not seen her for years. While we were driving, Greg said that he would leave his jacket in the car. Once we park, he decides to wear it. We enter the open, dark venue and stake a place near the front, behind the speakers. Greg brought ear plugs for both of us.

The band steps out and begins to play. The lead singer reminds me of the guy who used to run a local pizza joint in my hometown. Their clothes are plain and unassuming. Worn but not tattered jeans, t-shirts, and sweatshirts. The music begins. It is beautiful, forceful, melodic, woven. I enjoy watching the people around us. I notice two couples who each look like they could be brother and sister. One couple is quite tall. She reminds me of the singer Feist. She is wearing black fish-net stockings and a mini-skirt and a black, lace top. Somehow, this outfit works well for her. There is no smoking at the venue. We smell marijuana.

I am transfixed by the band. They are confident and relaxed. There is one woman in the band of three, her name is Georgia. It is tempting to say that her looks are plain, but they are not. Perhaps unassuming is better. I can tell that she is a force. She plays the drums, keyboard, and guitar. Maybe more – I couldn't keep track. She has a beautiful voice. She is married to the lead musician. I wonder what they do after the show.

At 11:30p Greg and I decide to go home. The band is still playing. As we walk out, Greg says that he likes the song. The night is still cold. There is still traffic on the way home, but no evidence of the accident. We pay the babysitter. She tells us that Belle snuck out of her room after we left. They played one game of mancala. The fire has gone out and the house is 65 degrees. We get to bed by 12:30a. My alarm is set for 5:30a.

Ice, Ice, Baby

Much like last weekend, this weekend started with another winter storm warning. Belle's school closed early on Friday, and the kids and I were home by 1p. We had 10 minutes of snowfall followed by about 5 hours of sleet and freezing rain. Before dinner, we found that the driveway was covered with ice and the kids could actually sled down it. After a few runs, Belle and Abe suggested we check out the hill at the bottom of our street to assess its sledding properties. I wasn't optimistic, but figured, "What the heck??" The hill was a shimmering, icy green – no snow at all. Ever the optimists, Belle, Abe, and our neighbor Thomas went ahead and threw their sleds down and hopped on. Low and behold, they went zooming to the bottom! Apparently ice covered grass is just fine for sledding. After running home for a wardrobe adjustment, the kids ended up sledding for at least an hour. We come home to hot chocolate and a fire, ahhhhh!

The next morning, the hill had frozen over again, and all the neighborhood kids were out this time. Our neighbor brought his old-fashioned sled with runners. The kids rode it down a frozen, steep path – laying on their bellies, head facing forward, chins a few inches from the ground. We were out for at least two hours. The poor hill was a sloppy, muddy, frozen mess by the end.

Saturday evening, Belle was bursting with excitement thinking about what she would write in her school journal on Monday morning. She wanted to write about two days of sledding, icicles, and hot chocolate.

Halfway Done!

Greg finished his 6th cycle of chemo yesterday. It feels momentous for him to cross the halfway point. For the past couple of cycles, he's noted some GI upset. He describes feeling queasy and unsettled, but he is still able to eat and get through the day.

Funny Boy

Abe makes me laugh.

He can put his shoes on himself, but often puts them on the wrong feet. Until recently, he was wrong much greater than 50% of the time, which made me wonder. Perhaps he liked the mixed-up feeling. Or maybe he liked the process of being corrected and getting them back on the right feet. Yesterday, he put his shoes on and came up to me. "Are these correct?" he asked. I said, "yes." He then crossed one foot in front of the other and said, "Are they correct now?" I just had to laugh.

Tonight, I put him in the tub and then stepped away to put his dirty clothes in the hamper. When I came back into the bathroom, he was kissing his reflection in the tub spout, repeatedly. He would lean over, kiss the spout, lean back, lean over, kiss the spout, lean back. Now that's some self-admiration!

Dandelions

I've been trying to think of an analogy for the thoughts rattling around my head for the past couple of days. What comes to mind is dandelions. Imagine life as a field. The day-to-day stuff is the grass – those things that we just do every day without much thought. The grass is eating, sleeping, brushing teeth, bathing, working, getting the mail, making dinner – what folks in the medical world call ADLs (activities of daily living). Sometimes, our day-to-day routine is broken up by an unexpected variation – nothing major like an accident or a birthday or a vacation – just some little deviation in our day-to-day routine that makes an impression.

Yesterday, we went with Greg's sister to the Carolina Tiger Rescue sanctuary. Greg rode his bike (30 miles!) and the rest of us drove. On the way there, Abe calmly and confidently said, "There's Daddy." Nothing in my vision registered passing Greg. Looking in my rear-view mirror, I didn't see a cyclist. Scanning my recent memory of the road, I couldn't come up with a cyclist. I didn't think that Abe was lying, but I also couldn't see how we could have passed Greg and I didn't notice. We talked about it briefly, but I basically chalked up Abe's comment to imagination or confusion or some other roadside deviation that didn't involve his father. Once we got to the tiger sanctuary, Greg wasn't there. I wasn't worried – partly because I've trained myself not to worry about Greg and his bike rides and partly because I knew that if Abe had in fact seen his father in some kind of distress, his comment would have sounded quite different. We signed in and Greg arrived a few minutes later.

Turns out that we did pass him on the road and Abe was correct. Greg had pulled a fair way off the side of the road – well off the roadside and away from the place where a bike would normally travel. Abe's little eye had caught sight of his Dear Papa. Even today, something strikes me how Abe noticed his Dad off the side of the road when nobody else saw him.

This event is a dandelion in my day-to-day field of grass. Relatively insignificant in the scheme of life, but it sticks out in my mind. Be they a weed or a flower or a magical poof that carries wishes into the wind, some moments break up my field of grass in a noticeable way.

Lent

Today begins the season of Lent for many. Greg was raised Catholic, I was raised Protestant. I do not remember doing anything for Lent growing up. When I was in college, one of my best friends, who was fairly agnostic, observed Lent as part of a family tradition. She and her father gave up all dessert and sweets for Lenten season. I did not join in her practice, but I was fascinated with her observance and dedication. She carefully and thoughtfully turned away bowls of ice cream and fresh baked cookies while those around her dug in. She and her Dad frequently talked with each other by phone and shared stories of chocolate chip cookies gone by. As I've gotten older, I've become more comfortable with integrating religion into my day-to-day life. I've come to appreciate the security of tradition and the ways in which religion helps us to form connections with others and to appreciate the comforts we may take for granted.

Our family decided to give up after-dinner dessert for Lent. During non-Lent time, almost every night after dinner, the kids forage the kitchen for a small helping of candy, cookies, or ice cream. One of our family rules is, "Healthy food first," which implies that something not-so-healthy comes second. Dessert has become part of our regular dinner routine. During Lent, we will cut out this part of our meal. We've decided that occasional treats are still OK – such as a cupcake during a birthday celebration or a chocolate chip cookie as part of a post-race spread. I recognize that our Lenten "fast" isn't much of a sacrifice, but it is a small action that we will take as a family to recognize this season in the church.

On day one, I am happy with our choice. Belle and Abe will take part of a long and rich church tradition. They will see that as a family, we have the power and ability to deliberately change some aspect of our day-to-day life. I hope they recognize that they don't need every single wish and whim met – they can choose to give up something of pleasure and will be just fine. Perhaps, they will have a better sense of what it is like to live without.

This past Sunday at church, the children did a fun activity to better understand Lent. Before the service, somebody handed parishioners bright pieces of paper printed with the word "Alleluia!" The youth minister explained that some times in the church are for loud rejoicing and celebration but that Lent is a time of quiet reflection. The children walked the pews, collecting the pieces of paper, and put them in a foil wrapped box. The "Alleluias" will rest there during Lent. When Easter comes, the children will open the box and it will be time again to rejoice and be jubilant.

Cycle 7 … or Not

Greg had his next check-up at the cancer center today – bloodwork, MRI, and meeting with oncologist. His sister Debbie met him and I didn't go. Greg's oncologist changed her clinic days to Tuesdays and Wednesdays, which is when I work. For his upcoming appointments, I'll shift my schedule so that I can go with him. In a weird way, I've found some comfort in the rhythm of his 2-month check-ups. For this visit, his bloodwork looked good and his MRI was stable. Debbie is over five years past her cancer diagnosis. She says that she enjoyed meeting the staff at the cancer center and she collected a lot of materials from the resource room. I sense that it meant a lot to her to be a part of the visit and meet his clinicians. Moving forward, she'll have a visual picture of the some of the people and places involved in Greg's care.

Greg was supposed to start cycle 7 of his chemo, but his medicine is being held up by insurance. The initial approval was for six months. I thought that the continuation of therapy past 6 months was approved, but it was not. Approval is expected to come in a day or possibly a few days. The oncology triage RN said not to worry, the chemo is still in his system and still working.

After the clinic visit, Greg and Debbie went to our local pool to take video for Greg's Kona Inspired video. After the pool, they went out to lunch. Debbie came home with a giant piece of chocolate cake which she offered to share. While we're not doing sweets after dinner because of Lent, chocolate cake for breakfast is still within our Lenten rules.

Cycle 7

Greg is on day 4 of cycle 7 for his chemo. He has some tiredness and stomach upset. Still, he is tough and continues to work, exercise, parent, and stay loving and patient.

God

Ten years ago, if someone said, "In ten years, you will be married with two children, living in North Carolina, and working as a nurse," I would not have been terribly surprised. If this person said, "In ten years, your daughter will attend Catholic School, you will use a wood burning stove for heat, your husband will have brain cancer, and you will have given an enema to a federal prisoner," I would have responded, "No fricking way." For all the events in our lives seemingly in our control, there are just as many we can in no way foresee. I cling to the way my home is organized, the food I prepare, and the calendars I plan each month. I also appreciate that much of life is beyond my direct influence. The world, the seasons, the billions of people – they swirl around me, beyond my reach. I cannot control them and, yet, their ripples find their way into my life in surprising and unexpected ways.

I did not expect to write about my husband's brain cancer. Once the words started forming, I definitely did not expect to write too much about religion. And, yet, I've found that many of my writings relate to experiences at church and include descriptions of faith in our home life. Like many, my relationship to religion is complicated. I was born a Quaker and raised in the Congregational Church. Not long ago, a dear friend suggested the possibility that I was Jewish in a past life. At times I have felt atheist and other times I have felt comfortably anchored by the teachings of Jesus. The apparent calmness of Buddhism fascinates me as do the many forms and stories of Hindu gods. I sometimes struggle with the magic and mysticism of the Bible – plants and animals that speak, angels who descend upon us with warnings or proclamations of joy, a virgin birth leading to an equally unexplainable resurrection, and on and on. I am completely baffled by the idea of taking the words of the Bible literally. My faith guides me and provides security only when I sift through the teachings such that the literal words on the page are woven into allegories that guide humanity towards kindness and compassion. Even so, at church, my soul quiets as I take in the warm candles, a sturdy cross, and hymns pouring out of the choir loft towards parishioners below. At its core, faith helps me understand what lies beyond my five senses and guides me to think about compassion, interconnectedness, humanity, love, anger, loneliness, and a soul left breathless.

I am comfortable in the pews of our local Congregational and Catholic churches. Each offers connectedness and a space to ponder the mystery of God. The Congregational church teaches that God welcomes everybody. Like the Catholic Church, our Congregational church is anchored in social justice, working tirelessly to identify solutions to poverty, hunger, mental illness, and low literacy. The Congregational church most often speaks of a loving and forgiving God. Sermons discuss ways in which Jesus stayed acutely focused on spiritual growth, material sacrifice, and kinship with those who suffer.

Our Congregational Church is sometimes criticized for only recognizing a God who is kind and loving. Less attention is paid to the angry, vengeful God who sometimes appears in the Bible. This angry God makes me nervous. Sometimes this God reminds me of an abusive parent – becoming enraged and full of fury at a child's innocent (or perhaps willful) mistake. A few Sundays ago, a parishioner stood to read Scripture. He read from Jeremiah 4:1-10. I won't write the whole passage here, but the lines include the following, "Raise a standard toward Zion, flee for safety, stay not, for I bring evil from the north, and great destruction. A lion has gone up from his thicket, a destroyer of nations has set out; he has gone forth from his place to make your land a waste; your cities will be ruins without inhabitant. For this gird you with sackcloth, lament and wail; for the fierce anger of the LORD has not turned back from us."

As the parishioner read, I thought, "Wow! This church is finally going to help me figure out what to do with the angry, vengeful God – the one full of punishment and fury." I waited in anticipation as the minister stepped up to the pulpit for her sermon. As she got to her place, she said something to the effect of, "Goodness, I have no idea what that passage was, but that is not the passage intended for my sermon today." Well, shucks. Turns out, the passage should have been Jeremiah 1:4-10, which brings back our kinder, gentler God. And, so, I was left wondering what to make of Christianity's angry God – the one who wields starvation, pestilence, and disease when Her followers go astray.

I do not believe in an Omniscient God, observing and guiding from a space beyond the day-to-day workings of humanity. A few weeks ago, Belle asked if God sees and knows everything. I said, "I don't know." Greg said, "Yes." (Perhaps I should have said, "No, only your Mother can do that."). Most simply, I believe that God is the hum and pulse of love and that Jesus is a physical manifestation of that love. If a cell is removed from our body, it dies. Within the fabric of our entire being, that same cell becomes a complex machine, the driving force of life. That is God. The memories left with others once we have died, that is God. I am very comfortable believing that God resides within each and every one of us.

In thinking about the recent Bible reading at church about an angry God, I realized that God's anger may not be so very different from my own – a welling of emotion based on a sense of betrayal or unjustness. Anger feels like an unhealthy emotion – one that results in hurt feelings and an elevated blood pressure. When thought of as an extension of God, perhaps anger serves a more positive role. Anger unburies words left unsaid, it warns that something is amiss, and when recognized and acknowledged, it generates motivation for change. If God is love, if God resides within our cells, then anger may be an expression of God designed to empower, enlighten, and cultivate change.

Bingo

On Saturday evening, we went to Belle's school for an evening of Bingo. I cannot remember the last time I played Bingo. In fact, I have no memory of ever actually sitting in a large room with a large group of people playing Bingo. Maybe I played it at some point in my life, or maybe I just saw it in a TV show.

Greg, Belle, Abe and I bought two packs of Bingo cards for the night and several slices of pizza. Instead of money, there was a table of prizes which people from the school had donated. Abe immediately honed in on a Star Wars Lego set. He became obsessed, talking non-stop about his Legos and when we were going to win his Legos. We tried several times to explain that it was not HIS Lego set and that we might not win. He could not accept our explanation and became hysterical at the thought of not going home with the Lego set. We tried to distract him by letting him draw on the back of the loosing Bingo cards (which worked, a little bit).

Apparently, there are lots of different versions to Bingo. Somebody wins in "regular" Bingo when the number/letter combos are called out such that the card gets five across, down, or diagonal. We played one round where the winning card had to create an "X" across the card. There is also something called "four corners" where you win by filling in each corner of the grid.

After multiple rounds, Greg won during a round of regular Bingo. Abe immediately dashed up to give the card to the caller, and without waiting even a nanosecond, bolted right to the table and grabbed his box of Legos. Oh, was he happy! Now, the pressure was on to win again for Belle. We went a few more rounds without a win. Before we left, they played a game called "worst card." For this version, everybody stands up. The caller reads the letter/number combos. Each time a letter/number is called, whoever has that combo on their card sits down. Last one standing wins. So, in order to win, the person must have the "worst card" with none of the letters/numbers called on their card. We all stood and the caller started calling out. After about seven or so calls, I was the last one standing – woo hoo! I had my eye on a colorful game called Connectagon Treetop. However, Belle really, really, really wanted a set of cheap neon earrings. Alas, I obliged and she grabbed the earring set for her non-pierced ears (I later learned that she wanted them for her stuffed animals).

We had a blast. The kids held it together and each was able to walk away with a wanted prize. We enjoyed an evening together of family game time. I was happy to have been a winner, even with the "worst card" (how's that for a life lesson?).

Nine Years

Greg and I celebrated nine years of marriage this week. In many ways, we're just doing what humanity has been doing for thousands upon thousands of years. In other ways, every moment feels wild and mysterious and uncharted. Either way, I am deeply grateful for the strength and security of our union.

Wednesday was our actual anniversary. My NC parents kept the kids through dinner, allowing Greg and me to enjoy a nice meal out. We went to a restaurant down the street where Greg had bratwurst and I ordered a Cubano sandwich. We also had a gigantic bowl of yummy onion rings. My parents kept the kids overnight last night so that Greg and I could enjoy a kid-free evening and morning. Initially, Greg and I planned to eat near the mall and then tackle some shopping that has been on our to-do list. The dinner plates we got for our wedding have a design flaw that we've just been dealing with for the past nine years. Greg thought that we should go ahead and finally replace our dishes. I told a friend that we weren't doing anything terribly exciting for our anniversary – just going to the mall. She kindly reminded me that a relaxing evening running errands without the kids, just strolling around the mall, is perfectly acceptable.

When I dropped the kids off at my parents, my Mom asked what our plans were, and I told her. She smiled, went to her purse, and gave me a knowing smile. As she handed me some money, she said something to the effect of, "Honey, go to a real restaurant and have a nice dinner. It's your anniversary! Go to the mall another time." Oh, Mom. I kissed the kids good-bye for the night and headed home. I told Greg that Mom had given us some money to go out for a nice dinner and off we headed.

At 5:30pm, we were the first patrons at the restaurant. I started out with a gin and tonic, where the gin was infused with cardamom (one of my favorite spices). I never drink gin and tonic, but this one was delicious – a mix of smoky and sweet, with the bitter of tonic. We ordered a tempura appetizer made with local vegetables – kale, sweet potato, and beets. Greg ordered gnocchi and I went for steak with sides of roasted broccoli and a sweet potato, blue cheese gratin. The restaurant wasn't crowded yet, and we enjoyed our tasty food and fine dining experience. We hadn't changed our clothes before we left – we were both in jeans and Greg had on his wood-splitting jacket and I was in a running shirt. Nobody seemed to mind.

After dinner, we decided to still go to the mall. We looked at a few options for dinnerware, but didn't make a purchase. Earlier in the year, Greg's office participated in something called the Smart Commute Challenge. He won a Macy's gift card through that event, which he used to buy some work shoes on our mall adventure. It ended up being a perfect evening – a romantic dinner followed by time together to do some of the day-to-day tasks that were on the back burner because of the demands of the kids.

Right now, Greg is in the front yard chopping some firewood and I'm writing. We'll go get the kids in a few minutes and then head over to Chapel Hill to support a friend who is shaving her head for a foundation called St. Baldricks. Through the foundation, she raised over $2,000 to support pediatric cancer research. Greg is also having his head shaved, to support her efforts. I am filled with gratitude for our nine years of marriage.

The Last Day

I once dated a fellow who proclaimed a "live every day as if it is your last" mentality. The idea is to avoid delaying goals or ambitions until it is no longer possible to achieve them. If you always wanted to swim the Barrier reef or play piano or plant a garden but say, "nah, I don't have the time or resources right now, I'll do it some other time," then those things may never happen. I get it … sort of. However, if I literally think about living each day as if it were my last, I quickly become riddled with anxiety. All my life's ambitions spin into a panicked mess. Did I tell everybody how much I love them? Did I eat the most delicious meal? Did I accomplish what I want professionally? Did I do everything possible to help Belle and Abe thrive in this crazy world? Did my muscles ache with pleasure as I hiked that last hike? That's a lot of pressure for one day!

I wonder if there is a converse mentality that goes something like, "live every day as if you will grow to be one-hundred years old." This approach sits better with me. I can take a breath and calm my thoughts. I imagine roots growing out of my toes and burying deep into the earth as my branches grow and divide and reach towards the skies. I am anchored and verdant, rings of brown hues wrap around me, marking the years. So much of what is important in life takes time. Building friendships. Growing families. Earning degrees. Planting gardens. Training for marathons. Creating art. Each of these activities takes patience and perseverance over weeks, months, and years.

Something that has come from Greg's cancer is my exploring the tension between living each day as if it were my last versus living each day as if I will one day celebrate my 100th birthday. Each scenario is possible and I'll never know which one holds true until that very last moment (and maybe not even then).

Soon after Greg and I got engaged, I realized that I needed to make the time and mental space to enjoy the effort that goes into planning a wedding. I tried not to get overly focused on the wedding ceremony and reception, and instead looked for joy in partnering with Greg in the planning process. We visited venues, met with the ministers, decided on colors and flowers, selected readings and music, and shared in the journey of joining together our lives and families. Not all of the planning went smoothly. We struggled with whether we wanted a large or small wedding. We argued with my parents about religion and center pieces. I ended up not liking my hair-do – piles of my thin, straight hair arranged into ridiculous curls held together by bobby pins and hairspray. Even with these difficulties, planning process was a time for Greg and me to connect and share. As we sipped on cold beer and discussed options for how to bring a Catholic priest into the congregational church I grew up in, we started the challenging and rewarding work of becoming a family. Our wedding day was glorious in every possible way (except for that darn hairdo). Even if the day had been filled with mishaps, by taking the time to enjoy the planning process, we helped ensure that our "I dos" had solid substrate beneath his tuxedo and my flowing dress.

I am much more comfortable living as if I have thousands more days ahead of me as opposed to only one. I relax, I plan, I dream big and long. Greg's cancer is a fishing net cast out into the deep, wide sea. We pull in other cancer stories. Some people are cured. Some live with their cancer for years. Some gasp their last breath within weeks of being diagnosed. These stories have always been around me, but now, they are more fully present. What was ethereal – a vague awareness that gray hair is not a birthright – has become more solid. The comfort of my deep, long roots is challenged.

I find myself looking more closely at the anxiety of my last day. I shift nervously thinking of unfulfilled dreams. My thoughts lead me back to my wedding and once again, I am calmed. I do not need to run a marathon, climb a mountain, and cook gourmet meals every day. I do not need each day to be filled with the uncertainty of unachieved goals. Instead, I can value and celebrate the small steps that are a part of becoming the person I want to be. The whole wheat bread with peanut butter in the toaster is enough. Wrapping a friend's birthday gift in newspaper is enough. Sitting down at our weathered, glitter crusted table with Greg and two wiggly, bouncy children is enough. Every breath, every heartbeat is a celebration.

The Blitz

We submitted and released Greg's video for Kona Inspired. My brother Noah produced the video. He and Greg worked together (with a bit of input from the wives) to pull together the images, text, and overall flow. The video shares pieces of his cancer story, interwoven with him swimming at our local pool, running on the wooded bike path behind our house, and chopping firewood in his Splish™ bathing suit with a rainbow, unicorn design. Whatever the outcome of the competition, the video is a celebration Greg's strength, character, and humor (who else could pull off shiny, rainbow decorated swim briefs while chopping firewood? Nobody I tell you, nobody).

When Greg first mentioned wanting to apply for Kona Inspired, I was cautious. I was still reeling from the punch of his diagnosis, surgery, and treatment. I was also aware of how intense and time consuming it is to train for an Ironman. Even with my hesitancy, my gut (and my voice) said "Absolutely, go for it!!" Our goals fuel our spirits. They pull us out of bed in the mornings and whisper or shout, "Come on, let's get going!"

I'm surprised at how fun and rewarding these first few days have been in getting people to view and vote for Greg. I get a charge every time I log onto Facebook and view the video and comments. It is great fun to watch the count go up for the number of views. Greg and I have each e-mailed dozens and dozens of friends and family to share the video link and ask for their vote.

Even though we are pleased with the current outpouring of support and the counts he is getting for the video, we are aware that his chances of winning may not be as high as we wish. The stories from last year's winners are compelling and dramatic – the videos are well produced and the winners are true testaments to the ways in which humans can experience a devastating set-back and come back through a journey of physical and mental strength.

We will ride this wave as long as we can (hopefully to Kona).

Cycle 8

Greg is asleep. He quickly fell into the deep, heavy slumber that hits him at the end of each chemo cycle. He picked through his dinner. Some food does not sit well now.

The Kona Inspired video is released and Greg's story is doing well in terms of number of views. Two new entries were posted today. Greg very much wants to compete in Ironman Kona. He talked about it long before brain cancer.

I'll go crawl into bed, next to slumbering Greg. I hope his dreams are bringing peace, unraveling mysteries, calming fears, lighting possibilities.

"I Hope They Make It."

Greg's video was posted to the Kona Inspired site in mid-March. For two weeks, he was the front runner in terms of number of views and, in my opinion, in content. Today, that changed. Today, four new entries were posted, two of which are stellar. The two new videos are emotionally compelling and well produced – a.k.a. slick. They are also about people living and thriving with brain tumors. Based on the winners from last year, Greg and I knew these videos were coming. Still, I somewhat guiltily confess, I'm bummed.

I saw the videos this morning and my spirit slumped a bit. I called Greg and said, "New videos are posted and they're what we don't want, strong competition." Inside, I was saying, "shit, shit, shit … ." Greg and I chatted for a moment and hung up. He called me back and our conversation went something like this:

Greg: *Yep, they're good, really good. I hope they make it.*

Me: *What? You hope they make it? To Kona????*

Greg: *Yes, they have very strong stories, they deserve to go.*

Me: *Um, yeah, I guess so…*

Kona Inspired has almost become a physical presence in our home. It is a welcome distraction, reminding us about what is good about the cancer experience. Weeks after surgery, Greg went back to work full-time, dedicated to his coworkers and projects. He has been a present and loving father – he goes to Mass with Belle every week, sits on our juice stained carpet and clips the children's finger and toenails, swims with them in the pool, and reads to them as night. He supports me and loves me in my endeavors. Our days are hectic, but once the kids go to bed, or before they wake up, he and I find each other for a quiet moment to connect, to talk and process the day. Entering the Kona Inspired program makes the most positive characteristics of Greg tangible.

In thinking about our very brief conversation this morning about the new videos, I realize that Greg's words capture his essence. Whatever the outcome of Kona, Greg's spirit is about nurturing and helping others. Greg has a strong fire in his belly to see this competition through to the end. Unlike me, his fire is in no way diminished by other people working to achieve the same goal, even if their win diminishes his chance of success. He pays witness to the stories and journeys of others who are living with brain tumors or other reminders of our mortality. He sees that like him, their stories are ultimately about harvesting ways to survive and thrive through difficulty. He is not petty or jealous or deflated. There are few people out there who are living with cancer, currently going through treatment, and are able to consider competing in the Ironman World Championships. Of this small pool, there are even fewer who have Greg's innate abilities to connect with and inspire others with humility, balance, and graciousness.

Risky Business

I am not a big risk taker. I have done some adventurous things in my life, like rock climbing and childbearing, but I did them with great planning, care, and deliberation. When I set out to try something new, I have fairly high confidence that I will succeed. Although I didn't really realize it when we started, Kona Inspired feels risky.

When Greg first mentioned wanting to try for the Kona Inspired competition, I was excited by the possibility that cancer might somehow create an opportunity for him to achieve an ambition. I also thought that it would be a big stretch for him to win. We knew from last year's winners that the competition would be strong. We (at least I) didn't have a full understanding of what would be involved in telling his story and making it competitive. We asked my brother to help, and he graciously and skillfully put together the video.

I don't remember where I've heard this saying before, whether from a movie or a friend, but the phrase that keeps coming to mind is, "We're in it to win it." Over the past few weeks, I've realized, or perhaps remembered, that I'm wired to work hard at something when I have confidence that I will succeed. I've also learned that my gut instinct is to back off of my efforts when the chance of success is diminished. If I don't try quite so hard, then perhaps the sting of defeat will be less painful. It is scary and unsettling to work hard for something that may not happen.

Greg is doing everything possible to win Kona Inspired. So far, he has tackled marketing cards, a professional-grade poster, grass-roots networking, newspaper interviews, speaking engagements, and a spot on a local news channel. A friend put in many hours of his own time to develop a website which both encourages people to vote and shares Greg's story. I am the 'cup-half-empty' person in the relationship, and I find myself thinking, "But he might not win … ." It's tough.

As I watch his video for the um-teenth-time, part of me is growing and changing. I am learning what it feels like, what it looks like, to go all out for something you want, no matter the odds. Kona Inspired makes me feel vulnerable.

I deeply want Greg to win a Kona spot. He is a man who had his head sawed open and part of his brain removed and then turned around and ran up a mountain. He takes cancer-fighting chemotherapy pills in the evening and then wakes up in the morning and cuddles with Abe and helps him get dressed. Sometimes the contrast, the intensity, the vulnerability feels unbearable.

In a way, the Kona competition is a fairly safe and fun way to experience the unknown – to dive into the feeling of going all out for something when the outcome is uncertain. I sense that in the years to come, there will be many more times when the path is unknown and when my instincts will want to pull back. I love that I am married to a man who is willing to put his whole self out there – to fight hard for what he wants. He doesn't hold back. It is beautiful to watch.

Easter

Belle and Abe were so excited about Easter. They set out their baskets, strands of plastic grass awaiting goodies to come, and Belle wrote a letter to the Easter Bunny. Below is the text of her letter and the bunny's response.

> Belle: *Dear Easter Bunny is it true that Jesus rose from the dead? And MyMom wants to know, is there one Easter Bunny for each town? love Belle* (at the bottom of the letter she put a sticker that said "You're a winner" and she wrote next to the sticker "Easter Bunny!")
>
> Easter Bunny: *Dear Belle, what good questions you ask! Jesus taught us how to love. Whenever you see love and whenever you show love, that is Jesus. Jesus is with you every day. As for your second question – let's just say that I have some help. With love, EB*

Easter morning, the kids tackled their Easter baskets and gifts from Greg's parents and we headed to church. We enjoyed a pancake breakfast and a service of communion, song, and reading of the story of Mary Magdalene and Jesus and the tomb. During communion, I was struck by a family sitting two rows ahead of us. There was a brother, the brother's wife/girlfriend, and a sister – each looked to be in their early twenties. They were sitting next to their father and the father's wife. After communion, the father was leaning forwards against the pew in front of him, hands covering his face. He was clearly in distress. His son was hugging him, rubbing his back. I was curious about their story. During the time for sharing gifts and concerns, the father stood and explained that his best friend was in a cycling accident and was likely going to die in the next day. His sorrow was palpable. With strong shoulders and tears streaming down his face, he explained what had happened to his friend and asked the congregation to take the time, even a mere 10 minutes, to cherish the people they love. His demeanor and testament were moving.

And so, another weekend comes to a close. We have a very busy couple of days before heading off on Wednesday for a family vacation. Greg is competing in a half-Ironman next weekend and we are going a couple of days early as family to relax and enjoy some time together.

In the News

We're at White Lake, NC today, getting ready for Greg's half-Ironman tomorrow. Our friends Dawn and Jim just arrived. They are checking out the digs. We'll be cozy and happy this evening! The water temperature for the swim tomorrow is supposed to be 52 deg – holy fricking coldness, yikes!!

An article about Greg and his Kona journey was written up in the local paper today, exciting!

Carolyn's Court

It is Wednesday afternoon, we are at Carolyn's Court in White Lake. We are staying in a 2-bedroom trailer and are unpacked and settled in. There is a set of bunk beds in the living room – Belle has claimed the top bunk and Abe the bottom. The setting is low key and relaxed. Greg calls our place "quaint." It is kinda cute.

My heart is bursting with admiration for Belle and Abe. In my 40+ years of living, I've had some fantastic travels. I've been to the beaches of Belize, Costa Rica, Cape Cod, Amelia Island, Bristol, and La Jolla. It would be very easy for me to scope out White Lake, NC and say, "Well, it's not as [beautiful, spectacular, breathtaking, romantic] as [some other place]." For Belle and Abe, everything is new and exciting and wondrous. We walked down to the lake after unpacking, and immediately the kids peeled their shoes off and were frolicking on the dock and along the shore. They ran after ducks. They kicked at the haze of yellow pollen collecting at the water's edge. They made footprints in the wet sand. They were free and happy and unbiased in that pure, unadulterated way that only children can be. Fortunately, their wonder is contagious. I can see our landscape through their eyes and enjoy the simple trailer and unassuming lake.

Greg is going for a 15-min run and I am putting dinner together – mac and cheese, hot dogs, beans, and broccoli. The kids are outside in a small courtyard, acting out an elaborate, pretend story of travels to

California and caring for homeless people. Belle is pretending to be a hotel manager and Abe is pretending to be a homeless person looking for a place to stay.

White Lake

Greg, Katie, Dawn, and Jim each finished the White Lake ½ Ironman on Saturday. Our first few days at White Lake were cold and rainy, but the brilliant sun emerged for race day. Friday night, we managed to fit 8 bodies and 4 bikes into our little Carolyn Court 2-bedroom trailer. In the early evening, we headed over to the race site for the pre-race meeting and pasta dinner. Greg set up a space to solicit support and votes for Kona Inspired. He made a slick poster and marketing cards to hand out, telling people his story and how to vote for him. In their usual form, the kids were happiest running, leaping, and stomping over a series of puddles near a pavilion.

On Saturday, the four racers were up and out by 7am. The kids and I stayed back to relax and clean up our temporary abode. This was Greg's first open water swim since his cancer diagnosis. The swim was 1.2 miles in very choppy, 54-degree water. Swimmers were required to wear wetsuits. Quite a way to get back into triathlons. I spent the day playing with Belle, Abe, and Addison while the athletes raced. We spent the day painting a birdhouse, finding food for lunch and snacks, and playing at the sandy beach near the lake. The kids and I cheered on the runners towards the end of the race. Greg, Katie, Dawn, and Jim all wore tired smiles at the finish. Everybody crossed the finish line in good spirits, good times, and with no injuries, yeah!

I found myself wondering how athletics and triathlons fit into the fabric of life and the human experience. In order to survive, we need to spend time on the basics of food, shelter, sleep, and sanitation. Most families need a paycheck, and job satisfaction is surely something to strive for. Once our basic needs are met, then loving relationships with friends and family feels most important to me. My spirit is fulfilled by connecting with and helping others. I enjoy sitting and reading with Belle, putting bubbles in the tub for Abe, sharing a meal with Greg, and discussing a new medication with a patient. It can be difficult to fit athletics into the mix of basic survival, work, parenthood, and connecting with friends, family, and community. Making time for a 30-minute run is one thing. Training for a triathlon is quite different. Each of us has

1440 minutes in a day – I question how many of those minutes should be spent preparing for an activity that doesn't directly connect with survival or work or helping others. When I am training for an athletic event myself, or when I observe others training, I sometimes ask, "what is the point of all of this time and energy?"

Watching the athletes finish on Saturday reminded me of the importance of exercise and competition and testing the limits of our spirit's physical home. My logical mind struggles to justify hours of training and participating in athletic events. However, my gut knows that the work of exploring the boundaries of our physical body is an essential part of being human – aching muscles and tender, swollen blisters can be grounding. Belle enjoys watching Greg's Kona video (she fancies herself famous). We've also watched a couple of the other entries and discussed the different stories presented. Last night, as I was putting her to bed, she asked, "Why do all of the people in Daddy's contest say, 'Anything is possible?' What does that mean?" I told her that the motto of the contest is "Anything is possible" and that the people submitting stories are showing that even if they've been sick or hurt, they are still strong enough to do a big, long race. Belle, who is both literal-minded and wants to challenge Mama when she can said, "Well, it's not true, anything isn't possible. People can't grow wings and fly. People can't change shapes into different animals. That's not possible." I was eager to get her to bed, so I just said, "Yes, I suppose you're right." I turned off her light and shut her door.

Today, I thought about what Belle said and realized that through exercise, people can grow wings and fly and change into animals. Perhaps not literally, but surely in spirit. We become weightless when we swim – arms and legs pushing against the water's firmness to propel us forward. Whether we become fish or frogs or floating leaves, when we swim, we forget about the 40% of our body that isn't water as our cells connect with the surface tension holding us up. Through simple mechanics, cycling allows us to glide over the ground, legs traveling in rhythmic circles, wind blowing against our face. Fields and flowers, buildings and bridges fly by – faster than our unassisted gait yet slower than a fossil fuel powered vehicle. When we run, for just a moment, both feet are off the ground and we sail through the air. For a mere nanosecond we are suspended above the earth, one foot having left the stability of the ground and the other foot waiting to arrive. Watching the athletes on

Saturday, I saw lots of tired, sweaty, fleshy beings. I also saw the triumph of our ability to transform our sitting, walking, lying selves into beautiful creatures that can stretch, float, push, wiz, glide, pound, and lift for miles and miles.

After the race, we loaded up the car to head back to Durham. Belle was ecstatic to ride back with Katie and Addison and Abe went back with us. Tired Boy conked out and slept for at least an hour, his little head tilted sideways as he drooled on the seatbelt. When we arrived home, we found that somebody had left gifts for us on our front stoop. A mystery friend left toy cars for Abe, a beautiful ceramic dish decorated with birds for Belle, and a gift certificate for Greg and me. A generous and unexpected surprise. Belle kept asking me to read what was on the gift certificate and asking who the gift was from. Here's our conversation:

Belle: *Who gave us those gifts?*

Me: *I don't know, the note doesn't say.*

Belle (after some serious thought): *Mom, I know who gave us those gifts.*

Me: *You do? Who?*

Belle: *Fairies. The fairies came while we were gone and left us those gifts.*

Me: *Belle – you are right! You must be right, the fairies did come and leave us gifts.*

Cycle 9: And the word of the day is ...

... stable.

Cycle nine of Greg's chemo starts this evening. It feels good to make tangible progress in his year of chemotherapy. This visit at the cancer center was the least eventful. Greg went through the usual steps – MRI, bloodwork, meeting with physician's assistant for neuro checks, meeting with oncologist to review everything, trip to pharmacy to pick up meds. Greg always makes people smile and laugh as he makes the circuit. Part of the neuro check evaluates short-term memory. The practitioner says three words, chats for a bit, and then asks the patient to recall the words. The less innovative practitioners use the same three words every time, the words from the mini mental status exam – apple, table, penny. They seem unaware that Greg is given these same three words about 80% of the time. Today, the practitioner says, "I'm going to give you three words. Then I'll ask you to repeat these words a little bit later." Greg says, "wait, wait, I think the cancer has given me ESP – don't tell me they're: apple, table, penny." The practitioner laughs, and then pauses a bit to try and come up with three different words.

Greg handed out cards with information on how to vote for him for Kona Inspired. One of the MRI techs moves the card forward and backwards in front of his eyes, having trouble reading the small print. Greg says with a big smile, "I think you need to make an appointment with an optometrist." The tech bust out laughing. I sometimes feel like a perpetual grump. Often, Greg's rays of sunshine drift my way and lighten my mood. The oncologist says that Greg's MRI is stable – nothing bigger, nothing smaller. This is a good thing.

This visit was also the first time I got the sense that our lives may at some point get back to some kind of normal. When the PA came into our room, she said that she just saw a patient with Greg's same diagnosis who has been off treatment for many years with clean scans. There will come a time when our only interaction with the cancer center will be an occasional MRI.

Angels Among Us, 2013

This past weekend was all about Angels Among Us, the annual fundraiser for Duke's Preston Robert Tisch Brain Tumor Center. We planned for and anticipated the event ever since Greg was diagnosed. Over 50 people joined the team to support Greg with fundraising and with emotional and moral support. With a financial goal set to raise $5,000, team Badousa Brain raised over $7,000.

A few weeks ago, Greg asked if we could borrow an extra jog-stroller for a family traveling from Colorado to NC for the event. We learned of this request through a connection at our local running store. The mom was diagnosed with Glioblastoma Multiforme (GBM) 13 years ago. GBM is the most aggressive form of brain cancer, with a 5-year survival rate of $<5\%$. She underwent surgery and treatment and has had clean scans since. We borrowed a stroller from a family at church. On Thursday, I called the mom from the Colorado family to discuss the logistics of getting her the baby jogger – she has a 1-y-old and 4-y-old. On Thursday evening, she left a voice mail saying that her MRI scan had come back clean – they were going out to dinner to celebrate.

The, "At Duke, There is Hope" motto can be read all throughout the Brain Tumor Center. I can feel cynical about hope. At times, hope is a cruel joke, tempting us into feeling good when doom is lurking in the corner. My cynicism evaporated as I talked with this Mom. She was the living, breathing proof of all that we want hope to be. For her, "at

Duke There is Hope" was somebody saying to her, "Your life is worth living. Even with a diagnosis of one of the deadliest cancers known to humanity, you deserve every possible chance to live the life you could leave without brain cancer." It was an honor to meet her, hear her story, and spend time with her family.

We woke up early Saturday morning. The Angel's organizers gave Greg table space at the venue to share information about Kona Inspired and solicit votes. He and friends left around 6a to go to the event and set-up. I woke the kids around 6:30a. It feels odd to use the words "brain tumor" and "festivities" in the same sentence, but for Angels Among Us, the words go together well. The event is set up not far from the cancer center. Activities included a 5K, survivor walk leading into a family walk, and stage presentations of music, recognitions, and remembrances. There were balloons and snow cones, flags and ribbons.

Participants are organized into teams, with a brain tumor survivor or victim at the center. There is a contest for the best t-shirt design, and there were many bright, rich images. The shirts were a mix of witty, funny, poignant, sad, and straightforward. The Badousa Brain team did each of the organized events – mingling, connecting, and sharing in the energy of the day. The kids and I walked the 5K while Greg ran at pace at the start of the race. He finished the race in less than 21 minutes on day 4 of his 5-day chemo cycle. The kids were happy running and walking along the course, enjoying the stream of people navigating the back roads of Duke's manicured campus. Although their stories were only quiet whispers on this day, several members of Greg's team are also living with cancer, some diagnosed within the past two years. I saw these survivors run in the event, torsos draped with our team shirt, and my heart was filled with admiration and gratitude. Greg walked in the survivor's walk, led by soulful, proud bagpipes. Families then merged in.

I talked to people living with brain tumors and to family members of survivors or of a loved one who died. Even with a clear and common theme, each story was different. From a clinical perspective, the brain tumor experience seems to be defined by where the tumor is located and how fast the cells grow. Tumors can be operable or inoperable. Some tumors are operable, but only part of the tumor can be removed. I talked with a woman who had a Grade 2 tumor that was completely removed. She does not need chemotherapy or radiation. I talked with a man with a Grade 2 tumor that is in the center of his brain, wrapped around important structures. His tumor is inoperable and he is undergoing chemotherapy. I talked with a boy who was diagnosed when he was 4 years old and has been undergoing treatment for the past 10 years. He has had multiple surgeries, radiation treatments, and chemotherapy. The tumor and treatments have changed his physical and cognitive abilities. At one point, his parents prepared for his imminent death. During Angels, he was in the children's play area with his family, in a wheelchair, telling jokes and engaging everybody around him. Surprisingly, nobody I spoke with described experiencing seizures. I heard stories of life-changing headaches, vision or hearing problems, changes in tactile sensation, and/or balance concerns. People felt safe explaining the details of that moment when they realized their lives would be forever changed. I started talking with one survivor and asked what type of tumor he has. He turned to his wife, eyebrows scrunched with trying to find inaccessible information, and said, "Honey, what is the name of my tumor type?" She looked at him, eyebrows raised, hand on hip and said, "Seriously?" It was funny. After just a few sentences, strangers turned into friends. The overall feeling of compassion and connection was immediate and profound.

Bursting

Spring is bursting round us. Our fridge is filled with strawberries from the market and we are planning to pick more at a local farm on Friday. We ate local, roasted asparagus for dinner twice so far this week. I took Belle and a friend to botanical gardens after school. Every bush, vine, and stalk was heavy with flowers – a multitude of colors, long and thin, short and round, tucked on the ground, swaying above in the wind, sweet scented, subtle, vibrant. At one point, the girls ran ahead towards a small cabin tucked along the edge of the gardens. Their feet darted lightly across a wooden bridge spanning a small pond. They paused, only briefly, to stare into the water below – the water was filled with suspended, black, teardrop shaped tadpoles, likely 20 per cubic foot. They admired the future frogs and continued on. After exploring the cabin, the girls found a nature trail leading to a stream. Off came the shoes and socks and they spent the next 30 minutes pretending to be baby tigers playing in the water. I spent my time looking for a 4-leaf clover. I'll keep looking.

The children are filled with good energy this week. They both have an air of relaxed confidence. Spring is breathing energy into their little spirits and they are breathing it right back.

New Rhythm, New Ride

Greg and I switched our schedule today. Usually, I bring the kids to school and Greg gets to work via bike, bus, or carpool. Today, I got up at 5a and walked up to the bus stop to catch a 6am bus to work. I was at my desk by 6:30a. Greg got Belle and Abe up, did their morning routine, and drove them each to their respective locations. He dropped the car off at my office and rode his bike to his work.

I loved walking to the bus stop as dawn was breaking. It was still mostly dark, with the slightest hint of daylight to come. The air danced with a mix of bird songs pushing their way through the morning caul. There were a surprising number of people out that hour – lights on in houses, cars driving by. I was never completely alone, and yet, the cool morning air held a stillness and quiet that I knew would pass as the morning rush-hour built.

The bus ride was enjoyable. More and more people got on the bus as it got closer to downtown. I relaxed and watched a different cast of characters hop on the bus. One man got on the bus with a black, vinyl work bag. He reached for his fare but then couldn't find it. He sat down, flustered, searching through his bag. He got up to chat with the bus driver and then sat back down. As soon as he sat down, he found his fare and everything about his energy relaxed. He went back up to the bus driver, fare in hand. With the bus swaying and bumping, he paid his due. He came back and started chatting with another passenger.

By 9:30a everybody in Family Sousa was where they were supposed to be for the day – on time and under budget. Being a one-car family can work, it just takes a bit of planning. Today, I appreciated the reward of a morning filled with new sights, sounds, and experiences.

In Greg's Words

The Magic of Belle

What a ride, er ah, day, today. I ran from Sunday service to home. Ran with Kona network cards for the off-chance. And Murphy's Law struck and had more worthy connections than I will recount here. On the American Tobacco Trail it included more than a handful of Sunday runners. One pair had already heard of me from a past campaigning activity, I was humbled. If we are to have a chance it is critical that I get a groundswell of local support rolling into Finals round. Another fellow had some knowledge of brain tumors, Tisch BTC, and my surgeon. He and his wife were from Canada and they saw my hat which had a maple leaf, courtesy of Liane T. They asked if I was Canadian which led right into Terry Fox. While chatting someone else stopped to solicit us for the July 27 Habitat for Humanity events. That person gladly received my Kona card with enthusiasm. That person's bike mate's wife is doing the Hawaii Half on Jun 01, and so the circle continues. I finally end my run and get back home. Then, family magic. I take Belle for a 1-on-1 trip. I have been quite cautious and aware to not over talk Kona in front of her. I need to stay alive for my kids, far more important than my athletic ambitions. My kids saw me during surgery, they were in the house for discovery, surgery, recovery. They saw, heard, smelled, lived EVERYTHING. I know that. Belle and I leave to do shopping for Mother's day, eat lunch together and do something we rarely do, spend time as a two-some. I put network cards in my pocket out of habit. We got to the mall and by chance parked next to a van. Out of the corner of my eye I caught their figures, lithe. I asked if they were endurance athletes stating I am one. They were interested, heard me and took a card. Short conversation, I have learned how to narrow the words. They moved on. Then, Belle asked if they voted for me. Having to think like a 7 year old I simply answered yes. To my surprise she did the classic fist-pump "yes"!!! And quickly said she wants to go to Hawaii and she has seen pictures of the water, beaches and flowers there, and on and on. So it hit me, just how much she is aware. Hmmm, another level of pressure on me? Nah. During our shopping time things just happened and flowed, we chatted folks about Kona when it was right and they mostly went really well. Perhaps it was Belle's presence and energy, who knows, but the web continues to grow, and we need it. By the end of our shopping Belle proclaimed we had exchanged with 34 people who would vote for us, "I'm sure" she says. Papa's heart was melting. Oh, the run today was a pleasant surprise, I am grateful to be building back more fitness.

Inspired

After getting the kids to bed, I saw an e-mail message from Greg's sister about the rules for the Kona Inspired contest. She said that she was confused because the rules for the contest were different from what she originally thought. I read her message and thought, "Oh, she must have somehow accessed the rules from last year's contest." I went to the Kona Inspired site and saw that the dates for submission were moved from May 7th to May 31st and the dates for the final round were pushed into June. This means that late entries can gather more votes and really late entries can still be considered.

Anger and confusion washed over me in a visceral way. How could a contest for one of the preeminent athletic events in the world change the rules on the last day of entry? A deluge of profanities came out of my mouth over the next 60 minutes. I huffed and cussed out to Greg who was putting his bike away in our bike shed.

I understand that the world is an unfair, unjust place. Lots and lots of unpredictable, unjust things happen. Duh. Still, I believed that a set of rules for a contest were a set of rules for a contest. It never occurred to me that the rules could suddenly and unpredictably change in a way that felt like a kick to the gut. Isn't a brain tumor enough? I thought that we had entered a contest for people with difficult life challenges to compete to win an entry into the Ironman World Championships – to show the world that the mind, body, and spirit are powerful and strong. Suddenly, I felt like I was in The Hunger Games, with The Capital manipulating the rules of the game to generate hype. Yuck.

Kona Inspired is tied to the Ironman World Championships which is run by The World Triathlon Corporation (WTC). We have known all along that WTC is a corporation and that this corporation developed and implemented Kona Inspired to promote its brand. Somehow, a little piece of me believed in the integrity of WTC – that they held to higher standards of conduct and sportsmanship. Nope.

Last night, I wanted to pull out. I wanted to say "F-it." Let's go to Costa Rica instead. Let's build a Terry Fox run in the Southeast. Why would we give any more time and energy to an organization that disrespects participants in such a way? Greg and I drafted angry letters to WTC. The clock ticked away. We went to bed.

And yet, for everything that has happened in the past 12 hours, Kona is still the pinnacle of triathlons. Greg is still a triathlete. Greg is still a brain tumor survivor. He is angry and upset about the sudden and unexpected change in rules. He is also committed to his goal of racing through the lava fields of Hawaii. He still dreams of crossing the finish line to the words of, "Greg Sousa, YOU Are an Ironman World Champion." He knows that if he gains a spot into Kona, he can achieve a life dream and he can use the experience to promote research for the treatment and cure of brain tumors. He stumbled but is not deterred. I want to quit. Greg is committed to persevering.

Mother's Day

My Mom, Mary Anna, aka Beme aka Mamacita aka Mafu Mommy celebrated her birthday a few weeks ago. I've heard it's rude to discuss a person's age, so I'll just say that the first digit of her new age is considered a lucky number and the second digit of her new age is naught. Just in the past month, she has planted her springtime garden, trained for and competed in more than one swim meet, finished the Angels Among Us 5K, tutored adult students in English, served on church committees, painted several impressive watercolors, and spent time caring for Belle and Abe. While nurturing herself, she also helps her four children in different ways. She (and my Dad) are very aware of and attuned to how hectic our lives are. They are always willing to pick Abe up from school, help Belle with homework, or drop off some goods from the farmers' market to contribute to our weekly meals. Sometimes, some yummy chocolate will magically appear on my kitchen counter. Thanks Mom! This weekend, my parents traveled to FL to spend time with my brother Ev, helping him with a life transition.

A couple of weeks ago, Family Sousa gathered at Noah and Yvonne's house with my parents for a combo birthday/Mother's Day celebration. My Mom and Yvonne have birthdays three weeks (and a few years) apart. Noah prepared a delicious salad dinner made with grilled steak, dates, blue cheese and an assortment of fresh vegetables. Dessert was the richest, most decadent carrot cake I've ever had. Whoever invented cream cheese frosting deserves Sainthood. My Mom got some rockin' gifts, including star shaped popsicle makers and a variety of 15 small cacti with thorns and brightly colored flowers. Even though it was a keynote birthday for Mom, she was happy with a simple gathering surrounded by family.

Today, Family Sousa spent much of the day making strawberry jam with the Schudels. We've made jam with them every spring for the past few years, so it has become a tradition. We picked our berries a couple of weeks ago and then stuck them in the freezer to keep until jam time. This was the first year the kids played together without needing constant supervision. The adults chopped berries, sterilized jars, mixed sugar into bubbling pots of berries, and lowered glistening red jars into a giant, boiling pot of water. The kids played music, dressed up like ladybugs, played on a rope swing, and decorated driveways with chalk. Everybody seemed happy and relaxed.

Last night Belle had a slumber party with a friend and we learned they stayed up past 1a (eek!). She missed out on breakfast this morning and is now asleep in bed. Greg is doing work, I am writing, and Abe and Thomas are outside being adventurers. Tonight, we will have a Mother's Day dinner to close out the weekend. I know that Belle and Greg did some shopping earlier this week, hummmmm. Tomorrow, another week begins.

Cycle Ten

It feels as if cancer is everywhere. Sometime lurking and sinister, gobbling up healthy cells and stealing vitality. Sometimes pushing its way into the core of our psyche, reminding us to grip tightly onto all that is beautiful and holy and loved.

Today, Greg learned that a friend died yesterday from metastatic breast cancer that spread into her brain and lungs. Earlier in the year, she traveled abroad to spend time with her dying mother. Within weeks of returning home, she was diagnosed with breast cancer. Despite treatment, the cancer took over. Her death shook Greg. He remembers spending time with her, listening to her voice. Greg thinks of her father, who lost a wife and a daughter within months of each other.

Yesterday, Angelina Jolie shared with the world that she elected to undergo a double mastectomy to reduce her chances of developing breast cancer. She carried the BRCA1 gene, giving her a >80% chance of developing breast cancer during her life. Her mother died from cancer at age 56. Jolie underwent major surgery to improve her chances at a longer, healthier life. She shared her story to generate important discussions around cancer and genetics. The last sentence of her article in the New York Times reads, "Life comes with many challenges. The ones that should not scare us are the ones we can take on and take control of" (May 14, 2013). I respect and admire her decision. I question the concept of control.

Tonight, Greg started round 10 of chemotherapy. The day started with him biking to the lab for bloodwork. In addition to his daily anti-seizure meds, he adds anti-nausea meds and the chemo pills during his cycle. He ups his intake of fiber (a full can of garbanzo beans with dinner this evening). He goes to bed earlier. Be still cancer cells, be still.

Doing Nothing

I have to tell myself that it's OK to do nothing. Doing nothing is different than doing something relaxing, like reading a book, collaging, cooking, or taking a bath. For me, doing nothing usually means zoning out on Facebook, watching Jon Stewart on Hulu, reading one of my Mom's People magazines, or rummaging through the kitchen to find an emotionally satisfying snack. If I were literally doing nothing, then I would be meditating, and that's actually hard work. The only real problem I have with doing nothing is that while I'm busy doing whatever nothing it is that I'm doing, the clock is still quite busy ticking away. In a perfect world, time would stop so that I could do nothing for a while and then pick back up with my constant, monumental to do list.

Hugs

Most mornings, Abe pitter-patters out of his room in his jammies. When he sees me, he leaps into my arms. His little arms wrap around my neck and his little legs wrap around my waist. He nestles his head into my neck and he relaxes. We stay like that for minutes. Our hearts separated only by skin and ribs. There is no better way to start the day.

FINALS!!!

Greg made it to the final round of the Kona Inspired competition!

Transitions

Today, we celebrated Greg's birthday and it was Belle's last day of first grade. Last year, Belle had a kindergarten graduation, caps and gowns included, so I clearly remember her last day of school. Strangely, I cannot sift through my memory to find Greg's birthday last year. He had his seizure on June 21st, 2012, so his birthday was a moment of calm and bliss before everything changed. Greg is not one for much pomp-and-circumstance. I imagine last year involved a family dinner and gifts, but my mind draws a blank.

There's a place in my heart that knows that today is a treasure – a collection of memories to hold onto. Another part of me feels that today was like any other – a rhythm and flow of familiarity. Tropical storm Andrea swept through our area today. I ran this morning in a gray, misty drizzle. Later, Andrea brought buckets and buckets of torrential rain. I ran errands with the kids, and when we got home, we were soaked. During the errands, the kids loved getting wet and had an intense need to change into dry socks multiple times. For some reason, I happened to have several pairs of dry socks in the car.

Belle's school let out at noon. She pranced out of school, just like any other day, with a backpack and a smile. We'd talked a couple of times this week about this being her last day of first grade. I know she was aware, but she was unfazed. First grade is in the past, and a luxurious, warm, firefly-filled summer awaits.

Greg's birthday was low-key. We ordered dinner from a favorite restaurant and ate as family on the porch. The kids and I hung a string of white lights and placed potted plants in the porch corners – splashes of purple, orange, yellow, and green. Greg was filled with love and gratitude.

Greg is off to bed. The dish washer is swirling. Only small drips of Andrea remain. I'm not sure what of this day I will remember next year. Right now, I am grateful for Greg, for Belle, for Abe, for summer storms that blow through fiercely and linger with gentle drips.

Cycle Eleven

Today starts Greg's 11th cycle of chemo. The kids stayed with my parents last night. We set the alarm for 5:15a. Greg biked to his appointments at the cancer center. I did my morning Facebook post to solicit Kona votes and then drove to meet him. We are used to the flow at the cancer center. While waiting, I went to the bathroom, where I saw a woman in a wheelchair and her husband right outside of the women's bathroom. The woman had thrown up – most of it made it into a plastic basin, but she'd gotten soiled as well. She was trying to get into the bathroom to get cleaned up, but her husband couldn't go in with her to help. She was weak and unsteady on her feet. I asked if she'd just had chemo. She said that she'd had chemo four weeks ago but still wasn't feeling well. I felt bad. I helped her walk into the bathroom and took care of cleaning the basin while she went to the sink to wash up. She kept saying that she was fine, but seemed more at ease once I told her that I was at the center with my husband, but I work as a nurse. She made it back out to her husband.

After the lab, we headed up to radiology for the MRI. I've always gone into the MRI room with Greg. The MRI tech asks him the same set of questions and then starts an IV. I sit and read a book while he lays in the MRI – 20 minutes of humming, whirring, popping, and clicking. The room is cold and sometimes I ask for a warm blanket. Greg lies in the sliding MRI bed, with his head locked in by a cage that goes around his head and over his face.

Next stop, Brain Tumor Center. Everybody sees Greg and immediately smiles. Greg gets his vitals checked (resting heart rate of 54 – wow!) and then we go into an exam room. We meet with a mid-level provider first and then the neuro-oncologist. Today, the provider insisted that she'd treated Greg before, but we had no memory of meeting her. We just nodded and smiled.

After she left, we waited for what felt like a long, long time for the doctor to come in. She has great bedside manner – she focuses on Greg, speaks clearly, and answers any question. Her manners and words felt different to us this visit. She is generally a serious person, but she has a warm smile and Greg can usually get her to laugh pretty quickly. She seemed less bubbly this time. She said, in her lyrical, Indian accent, that Greg's MRI looks "relatively stable." She talked about cells at the edge of the surgical incision. From what I've gathered, healthy cells healing from surgery can look like cancer cells on an MRI. The oncologist pays close attention to what is going on along the border of the surgical incision. She commented that they are looking at the cells along the edge of Greg's incision. She discusses this at every visit.

After briefly discussing the MRI, she talked about scheduling Greg's PET scan. This scan uses radioactive glucose to highlight active cancer cells. Greg will have the PET scan in August. The results indicate whether or not Greg comes off of chemo or needs additional treatment. She said that he may continue with chemo and may need radiation. We've known that there is a high chance Greg's cancer will eventually grow back. Our understanding was that Greg could go many years before any additional treatment. The doctor said that Greg will definitely need radiation in the future, with the future being 6-months to 6-years. The information she shared gave us pause. We asked a couple of questions, but weren't really sure what to ask. She explained that they try to delay radiation as long as possible and went over some of the side effects of radiation. I had the sense that something had changed in the assessment of Greg's tumor, but that the PET scan is needed to evaluate and make decisions.

As we wrapped up the conversation, a Code Red was called for fire and we were asked to leave the building. Patients and staff headed out to the hall, but there was confusion about what we were supposed to do. There is not an obvious staircase by the Brain Tumor Center and people weren't sure about taking the elevators. There were a few folks in wheelchairs. While we were all bumbling around trying to figure out what do to, the fire alarm was called off. Greg and I went to the front desk to schedule his August appointments.

Last stop, pharmacy. We are now used to confusion in the process of sending the chemo order down to the pharmacy. When we got to the pharmacy, the staff person said that their network was down and she didn't know how long we'd need to wait. We headed over to our favorite trail for a run. Greg ran two laps, I ran one, and we ran against each other, giving high-fives each time we passed each other. The morning air was dense and moist. The ground was wet with all of the recent rain. I ran some, walked some, happy to be surrounded by dense, lush vines and trees. We met back at the car and had a woman take our picture. We gave her a networking card to vote for Greg for Kona.

We went back to the pharmacy. Our favorite pharmacist greeted us. She asks about Belle and Abe and how summer is going. We've learned a bit about her life over the past year. She celebrated a key-note birthday and chose to spend her birthday on a humanitarian trip to Georgia (US) to support a non-profit agency called Fugees Family. Over the year, she is doing 50 acts of kindness to help and support others. She has helped and supported us over the year.

Summer Silence

"Give sorrow words; the grief that does not speak whispers the o-er wrought heart and bids it break."
~ William Shakespeare, Macbeth

There are many words I could write about Kona Inspired right now. Learning that Greg did not make the top two in his bracket was heartbreaking. There is no explanation as to how his leader-of-the-pack view count translated into a sub-second place vote count. One of the winners had less than ½ the views of Greg. Since the announcement, there have been a few small developments, heartfelt words exchanged between friends and family, a tear or two. However, for now, the contest is still ongoing. There is the possibility that Greg could win a spot via the wild-card option.

Greg finished his chemo on Sunday. It was a roller-coaster day – Father's Day, unexpected news from Kona Inspired, and the end of Cycle 11 of chemo. He started the day with a 60-mile bike ride with friends. We learned about the Kona results at lunch and were immensely distracted. The four of us sat on the porch at lunch. My mind was swirling with the confusion of the Kona announcement. Greg also seemed distracted. After lunch, I took the kids to a swim lesson and Greg met a friend to help chop and process a fallen oak. We celebrated Father's Day during dinner. We ordered carry-out from a near-by Asian restaurant and shared a few small gifts with Greg. He was utterly exhausted and melted into bed by 8p.

June 21st

Today is exactly one year from the date of Greg's seizure in Alabama.

Today is our neighbor Lauren's birthday.

Today is the summer solstice.

Earlier this year, we were trying to plan a family get-together in June to recognize two family birthdays and Father's Day. Greg said, "Well, June 21st is National Seizure Day." I believed him. There's every other kind of ailment day, why not seizure? My parents got his humor and laughed.

Alas, our neighbors are out of town today, so we cannot wish Lauren a Happy Birthday in person. We'll find a way to recognize her day of birth. We love our neighbors. Our kids play together happily (mostly) for hours and hours. The adults have much in common personally, professionally, culturally. We've been together for births and breast feeding, birthdays and block parties. We've shared hardships and frustrations. Michael and Lauren have been side-by-side with us, literally and figuratively, through Greg's cancer. They participated in Angels Among Us and solicited votes during Kona Inspired. They've been gone for a week and we're ready for them to come back to town.

June 21st the Summer Solstice. I have fantasies about creating idyllic family rituals to recognize summer and winter solstice, fall and spring equinox. So far, they haven't translated to anything beyond my imagination. Last night, I played around on Pinterest for a bit to see if I could find something quick and easy for us to do this evening. Lots of great ideas involving wreaths of flowers, homemade candles, spirals and circles made of pebbles, small homemade fairy dolls made from wood and felt. Maybe next year. Fortunately, Belle and Abe's preschool spends time on seasonal rituals – songs and crafts to recognize the beauty each season brings. Maybe tonight I'll make milkshakes. I may run to Duke's farmer's market later to buy flowers. We can stay up late and watch fireflies from the porch.

Blueberries

I love picking blueberries. I picked with my family when I was a little girl. We'd drive out of the city to one of the small towns outside of Gainesville, FL. We'd pick for a few hours and head home with our bounty. We would nibble on handfuls and then my Mom would freeze the rest for pancakes, muffins, and snacking. As a teenager, groups of us would drive out to the patch on a hot summer afternoon. We'd pick for a while and then drive to a nearby lake to swim. Those afternoons picking berries anchored my summer. I marvel that those little berries can find a home from Florida to Maine.

There is a blueberry patch less than 5 miles from our house. Two years ago, Greg and I took the kids picking. It was kind of a bust. Abe had no interest in picking at all – he ran around acting coo-coo. Belle didn't like the heat, didn't like the sunscreen, didn't want to wear her sunhat, and decided that all the berries were sour. After that trip, I was kinda sour too. Last year, Greg had his seizure before we could go to the patch as family again. I did go picking, though. The kids were in Rhode Island with Grami and Grampy. Greg was at work. The morning of my birthday, I decided to go pick by myself. I remember the morning sunlight skating across the bushes. I remember feeling very sorry for myself. We met with the surgeon that afternoon. He explained the pros and cons of surgery. I appreciated that he gave us the option of not having surgery (the tumor would likely grow and Greg would likely continue to seize). Sometimes doctors forget to explain what seems obvious.

This morning, I went back to the patch and Greg stayed home to wrangle the kids. The morning was warm, but not too hot. I wasn't distracted by making sure that Belle and Abe were comfortable and not disturbing others. There were already 15 - 20 cars parked. I grabbed a bucket and headed into the neat rows of bushes. Everything about the blueberry is perfect – its deep purple-blue color, its round shape with a crown on top, and its bursting sweet-sour taste of summer. A glorious orb of nutrition and divinity. I love the plunking sound the berry makes as it hits the bottom of the pail. The first berries make a satisfying plunk as they hit the bottom of the pail and then, after the first couple of layers, they nestle in with their friends in merry silence. I picked five pounds in just over an hour. My bucket was full and I was happy.

Countdown

This morning, Greg went to the lab for his Cycle 11, 21-day blood draw. Normally he bikes, but it was POURING rain – as in flooding, shallow-rooted trees toppled kind of rain. Duke switched to a new system for electronic medical records, so the lab could see his appointment but not the actual order. We had to wait a bit so that they could contact the oncologist for the actual order. We're home now, cleaning and packing for our flight to Rhode Island tomorrow.

Rhode Island

We are home from Rhode Island and settling back into life in North Carolina. Our time up north was fun-packed and busy, busy, busy. Those folks in RI sure do know how to par-tay! Our celebrations started on the 3rd. We headed over to the mall at 10am for Belle to get her ears pierced. After this monumental milestone, we went to Rod's Grill for lunch– a local diner we eat at every year. Rod's does not have a website and they do not accept credit cards. Despite a menu that includes soups, salads, and sandwiches, Rod's is best known for its wieners (no, not hot dogs, wieners). Their culinary glory is best appreciated when ordered with "the works" - meat sauce, diced onions, and mustard. After making the dreadful mistake of ordering a chicken sandwich on my first visit to Rod's in 2003, I now know to order the wieners with fries (I do believe I narrowly escaped being disowned by Greg and his family over that chicken sandwich fiasco).

After lunch, Greg and the kids got haircuts – Debbie's hairdresser fit them in during an unexpected cancellation. In the early evening, we braved bumper-to-bumper traffic to go to the carnival in Bristol. It is a small, local carnival with an assortment of rides, games, and glucose elevating food. We spent waaaaaaay too much money on rides, a game of shooting a cork gun, and a game of pitching bean bags into toilet seats mounted along a wall. We walked away with two packs of silly bands, three water guns, a whoopee cushion, a bottle of invisible ink, a small stuffed dolphin, powdered sugar-coated hands, and lots of good memories. As dusk approached we left the glowing lights of the carnival and headed over to a local fireworks display.

Unlike the wide, sandy beaches of North Carolina, the coastline of Rhode Island is jagged and rocky –inlets, spits, and coves weave their way along the space where land and water meet. Because of this geography, towns and neighborhoods often have their own dedicated beach areas that vary in size from a few dozen feet to maybe one quarter of a mile. Some are private and some are open to the public. A friend of Debbie's invited us to a firework display at his neighborhood's beach. We parked up a hill and walked a couple of blocks down to the water. There were about 50 people gathered. Besides the fireworks, a highlight of the evening is a large bonfire. There was a stack of wood pallets at least 10 feet tall with a fire truck a few feet away. A few children were playing in the water. We milled about enjoying the excitement and the intimacy of the gathering. Some children handed out glow sticks. The sun set and the fireworks started to fly. The show was impressive – booming, contrasting blasts of light and color lit up the night sky, shooting up and exploding over the water. The bonfire was lit and everybody cheered. Small fireworks were imbedded in the wooden crates, making loud pops as the fire consumed the wood. We left after a full 20-30 minutes of fireworks and they were still going strong. Home to bed.

The next morning, we drove to Bristol for the parade. Every year, I am struck by the number of people (~200,000!) and the varied and creative combinations of red, white, and blue. Instead of the usual double yellow line, the center line of the parade route is a stripe of red, white, and blue. People show their patriotism through flags, banners, flowers, shirts, hats, hair ties, toys, costumes, cars, hair die, face paint, jewelry, socks, and probably underwear (I didn't check). I even saw a couple of red, white, and blue painted pets. The parade has beauty queens, marching bands, town officials, antique cars, scout troops, military servicepersons, police and fire workers, horses, bikes, floats, and even cannons. The parade's revelry and patriotism show how a small town can come together in a big way.

After the parade, we went to the house of a friend of Grami's for one heck of a party. Belle and Abe were happy to swim in the pool while Greg and I alternated between swimming with the kids, eating, and visiting. I won't list everything, but the party included four tables of food, four coolers, a DJ, and Jell-O shots. Remember, this party was hosted by friends of the grandparents, not the kids – when was the last time you were at a party with Jell-O shots?? At one point the 65+ crowd was singing karaoke and shaking it under the gazebo. Party guests included family and friends from Greg's childhood. Lots of people wanted to give Greg a hug and catch up. We left the party in the late afternoon, feeling the need to get home and unwind a bit. Our four-pack went to bed early while Grami and Grampy headed back out to the party to catch their firework display. Quite the party animals!

July 5th was relatively calm. We went for a nature hike down to another inlet and shopped for a picnic gathering on the 6th.

On the 6th, Greg's family organized a picnic for friends and family at Colt State Park. Debbie reserved a spot in a shaded, woody area. We spent time with family friends, Greg's Godparents, my friend Deb who drove over from CT, and lots of Greg's friends from college and his

BMX biking days. The crowd ranged in age from two to almost ninety. We mingled, ate, and relaxed under the trees. Later in the afternoon, Greg's friend Kevin brought out his bike. He is still an active rider, well known for his adventure and skills. He managed to convince 5 or 6 of the guys to lie in the road while he jumped over them with his BMX bike – no ramp. I'm sure he's done the trick a million times, but it's still nerve racking to watch him sail over living, breathing bodies. It's hard to keep the imagination from exploring the crunch of wheels and metal on flesh (hence, part of the allure). One of the fellows was a few months out from major surgery to repair a shattered tibia he injured biking. After jumping over his friends (he landed safely), Kevin's two-year-old son lay in the road and asked Daddy to jump over him. Some Dads throw their kids in the pool, some swing them in the grass, and some jump over them with their bikes. Abe caught wind of what was going on and, having no idea what he was getting himself into, ran over to his new friend and skidded on the dirt road to lie next to him. Kevin peddled towards the boys and easily sailed over their little bodies. Phew. The end of the afternoon included lots of bikes and dirt. One group of kids tucked themselves away in a grassy area and worked on tackling a variety of elaborate Rubik's Cubes. We eventually traded our last hugs and packed up and headed home.

The night of the 6th, Greg's Uncle John hosted his annual family gathering in his backyard – bonfire, sparklers, and fireworks included. Uncle John and Aunt Terry live next door to Greg's parents, so going to that gathering involves walking out the back door and across a grassy field. Uncle John and Aunt Terry have eight children, so their family gatherings are large. The adults set up a circle of chairs around the bonfire and the kids ran and jumped and played, spinning with sparklers. Grami brought fixin's for s'mores. The smoky, warm, gooey sugar wrapped in crunch is just soooo satisfying! We watched another round of fireworks and headed off to bed.

The morning of the 7th, we went out to breakfast with Greg's parents before driving over to the Cape to visit my friends Bobbe and Dave and my Aunt Joyce. I lived with my Aunt Joyce and Uncle Lee when I was in the third grade. Uncle Lee died from a brain tumor in 1995. I can picture his smile. He taught me how to make pound cake from the Little House on the Prairie cookbook. I have a set of three small, ceramic elephant figures he brought me from an overseas trip. Bobbe is one of my

Aunt Joyce's best friends. I lived with her one summer in college when I was doing research at Woods Hole. It was a luxurious summer. Bobbe filled the role of both friend and mentor. Her house sits tucked up on a wooded hill, overlooking the ocean. She and I shared many meals together – sitting at her breakfast table looking down the hill to the water. She taught me to sew and helped me make a summer dress of dark blue batik fabric. For the 4th of July of my summer on the Cape, Bobbe and her sister and friends took me on a boat to watch fireworks from out at sea. Later in the summer we sat through a hurricane together. Driving around after the storm past, there were large sail boats that had been lifted out of the water onto lawns and roadways.

It is only an hour's drive from Greg's family's house to the Cape. We arrived just before lunch. Belle and Abe immediately set out to explore the yard and tackle a Play-Doh set out on the porch. Seeing Bobbe and Aunt Joyce now is bitter-sweet. Bobbe's son Jamie died suddenly and unexpectedly in 2011. My cousin Sherrie, Aunt Joyce's daughter, died from breast cancer in 2008. There is a shadow of stillness and gravity to a parent whose child has died. Bobbe showed me a photograph and a painting of a memorial site dedicated to Jamie. The photograph was taken on his birthday, there is a giant rainbow arching across the sky over the site.

After lunch, the four Sousas and Aunt Joyce headed down to the beach. It was crowded, but the water was perfect – cool but not cold, wavy but not overwhelming. We found a spot on the sand and Belle and Abe ran and played in the water. Belle was braver than Abe and confidently walked out into the water, jumping up and smiling with each wave. Greg watched the kids and I talked with Aunt Joyce. The summer I lived on the Cape, I loved collecting stones from the beach. The smooth, round stones vary in size and are a mix of pink, orange, white, gray, black, and yellow. They look like jewels sitting at the water's edge, turning duller as they dry. Finding a stone with a contrasting ring of color around it is considered good luck. Belle remembered this from our last trip to the Cape and set out to look for lucky stones. We played for an hour and left when we heard the rumble of thunder. Back at the house, we ate homemade blueberry cake and then headed home to Greg's parents.

Our last day, we enjoyed time with friends and with Grami, Grampy, Auntie Debbie, and Cousin Zachary. We spent the afternoon at our friends, the MacDonald's – the kids ate popsicles and played on a slip-and-slide and the parents talked about biking, parenting, and summer adventures. For dinner, Greg's friends Dave and Andrea and their son Ruben drove down from Worcester, MA. More swim time, more food, more catching up and reminiscing. Greg's family was so good to us over the week. They fed us and loved us and made sure we were comfortable. They spent time with Belle and Abe while Greg and I ran each morning. The week was intense and fun. We came home with memories of fireworks and water, with a new set of pierced ears and a red-white-and-blue hair tie, with hugs and kisses from friends and family, and with a bag of lucky stones collected from the shore.

Cycle Twelve

Greg started Cycle 12 of chemo today. He was supposed to start yesterday after his bloodwork, but there was a communication delay between the oncologist and the pharmacy. We have come to expect gaps in our health care system and no longer get flustered. I finished up a home visit for work and then went to the cancer center pharmacy to pick up his meds. I felt a strange sense of comfort as I walked from the heavy, damp air through the sliding glass doors and into the cool, stone lobby. We have gotten to know many people–help staff at the front desk, MRI techs, phlebotomists, cashiers at the coffee shop, RNs, oncologists, and pharmacists. They have all been with us during Greg's treatment.

We hope and expect that this will be Greg's last round of chemotherapy for a long while, hopefully many, many years – maybe forever. We hope that the chemo pulled the plug on whatever cancer cells remained after surgery – their devious engines robbed of the fuel and mechanics of perpetual growth. The cancer center will still be a regular part of Greg's life – with MRIs every few months, eventually annually. Some of the medical staff may stay a part of Greg's treatment. Others will move onto new places, have children, explore new careers. The cancer center remains. For me, now, the flickering blue-gas fire across the back wall of the lobby, the grand piano at the bottom of the ground floor, the shimmering granite floors, the wig store, the meditation room, the library, the small key-pad lockers in the MRI waiting room – each carry a sense of familiarity, caring, comfort.

Greg prepares for a week of tiredness, for a week of slow-moving bowels. When I go to bed at night, I will listen to his stomach churn and grumble. Not too much else will change. He will still work, run, parent, and be present.

Today is exactly one year from the date of Greg's surgery. Last night, Greg reminded me that on that night one year ago we were on the 9th floor of Duke's main hospital. His head was adorned with strange greenish-blue orbs. We had no idea what lie ahead. Next year is a mystery. We only have glimpses of the path. We step forward, one day at a time, hoping that comfort and blessings and joy await.

What's Around the Corner?

Today, Greg and I met with the Angel's Among Us organizer to discuss ways to help support the Brain Tumor Center. We've got ideas and need to shape and mold them into a form. Kona Inspired felt so concrete and tangible. Poof, gone.

We're in an odd space with Greg's cancer. He's finished his year of treatment, but we can't really do much until he gets the PET scan in August. He has been ceremoniously getting rid of the foil wrappers his chemo came in. A few went in the trash at the Triangle Triathlon. Take that, chemo!!

Flip Flops and Sneakers

You know you're headed into a fun weekend when the only shoes you need to pack are flip-flops and running shoes. Our next-door neighbors have a family home on the Neuse River and we are blessed to receive an invitation.

The Rivah'

Our weekend at the river was fantastic, only too short. To get to the River House, we wind our way from the interstate to a highway to a 2-lane rural road to a dead-end gravel drive, passing tobacco fields and fruit stands along the way. There is a small collection of waterfront houses along the estuary, with open, green space behind them. There are fig, pear, apple, and peach trees. There are blueberry bushes (my fingertips pulse with the picking potential as we pull in to park). In mid-summer, most of the houses have gardens bursting with peppers, tomatoes, and okra. There is a sandy beach along the wide, brackish water. A hurricane tore down an old wooden dock a few years ago and the homeowners came together to rebuild a strong, sturdy, cement dock.

Shoes come off after parking the car and there's really no need to put them back on again.

The house we stay in is luxurious. It belongs to the parents of our next-door neighbors and has been in their family for decades. A few years ago, they tore down the smaller one-story home and built a larger, modern, two-story home. Everything is open, light, and welcoming. For sleeping, we put all four kids together in one room and each set of parents got a room. We drove in Friday evening and let the kids run around while we unpacked. It was late by the time we got everything and everyone settled (10pm is late, by Sousa standards).

The kids were all up by 6:30a on Saturday morning. They went out to the beach and played in the water for 5 – 6 hours, almost non-stop. There is plenty for adults to enjoy at the river – relaxing on the porch, walking, sitting on the beach or dock with a beer, picking fruit, and swimming. This trip, I found that much of the fun came from soaking in the kids' complete, unfiltered joy. Unstructured play is quite miraculous as their little bodies and minds explore the world around them. We all enjoyed dinner together on the porch and spent the evening mingling with neighbors. There was a steady breeze and no bugs. Sunday was more play time and we all headed back to Durham around lunch time. We could have spent many more days there.

Back in Durham, Greg and I went to the screening of a documentary called "Within Reach: Journey to find Sustainable Community". It is about a couple who quit their jobs and decided to bike across the country to visit and learn about sustainable communities. We enjoyed the movie and time away from the wee ones. I am struck by ways in which modern humans in the developed world work to balance our basic needs of food and shelter with our spiritual needs of love and compassion with the complexities of modernization and technology. Like the subjects of the movie, Greg's next adventure may include extended time on a bicycle, working to schmeer some Badousa Brain love across the bagel of life.

Irony, Beacons, and Sunsets

Cancer causes trouble because it grows and grows with reckless abandon. Damaged cells divide and replicate, crowding healthy cells and disrupting their ability to do their jobs. Once cancer has taken hold, lung cells cannot process oxygen, lymph cells cannot fight infection, liver cells cannot clean toxins, brain cells cannot serve as central command. Curing cancer means learning how to stop these cells from their ceaseless dividing and migrating. Skloot's book, *The Immortal Life if Henrietta Lacks (Crown Publishing Group, 2010)*, traces the journey of Ms. Lacks' cervical cancer cells. Ms. Lacks' herself is long gone, but her cancer cells are still around. Thousands of laboratories around the world house cultures of her cancer cells as they continue to divide and replicate, no end in sight. One of humanities most desirous achievements is stopping the never-ending dividing.

Our brain is the essence and infrastructure of who we are –home to our thoughts, our personality, our wishes, our fears. We are not our breasts or our livers or our lungs or our bones. We are our brains. Brain tumor patients struggle with the fear of a cancer diagnosis and with the awkwardness of an unwelcome guest shoving its way into that which holds memories, processes color, scent, light, and guides our moods and movement. They are forced to identify and hold onto the pieces that that have not been disrupted.

This morning, Greg shared with me the death of a local brain tumor patient. He was 29 years old, married, with a one-year old son. He was diagnosed with Glioblastoma Multiforme 8 months ago. Before cancer, he was lean, athletic, handsome. Over the months of treatment he became puffy, swollen, sagging, non-ambulatory. I remember him from Angels Among Us. This was our first Angels and it was also his first. Tonight, I think of what his wife wrote in the days before his death. He asked to have his hospital bed moved so that he could look at the sunset. "God is good" were his words. I sense from his wife's writing that his death does not diminish these words in any way.

Super Belle

Greg woke up early and headed out for a short run. He's training for the Bridger Ridge Run in Bozeman, MT on Saturday. I took the kids to school and Greg biked to the lab for a round of bloodwork. We're hoping that this is the 2nd to last bloodwork for a while.

Belle did her first triathlon this past weekend in a series called Kids in Training. She swam 50 yards, biked 1.75 miles, and ran 0.3 miles. She is not on a swim team and doesn't have much practice swimming any distance (handstands in the water, now that she can do!). We were a bit nervous about the 50-yard swim. She took on the whole race with a great attitude and lots of gusto. She finished the race, earned a big medal, and had an awesome smile on her face at the end.

Tomorrow, we're off to Montana. Greg has the Bridger Ridge Run on Saturday, but otherwise we hope to relax and enjoy the ranch and time with my parents.

Montana

My birth certificate documents that I was born at 9:09pm on June 28th, 1971 at Bozeman Deaconess Hospital. My parents moved from Montana to Utah soon after I was born, divorcing when I was two years old. I went with my mother to Gainesville, FL and my dad returned to Gallatin Gateway, MT to live. I have no early memories of MT. The first trip I remember making to MT was when I was ten. I then flew from FL to MT every summer to visit my Dad and stepmom, Gramona, for a week or so.

One of my Dad's greatest passions is moving water around his arid property. Montana rivers, filled with snow melt and rain, are diverted into irrigation canals for crops and livestock. Decades ago, my Dad paid a year's salary to secure the oldest water rights in the county for the canal on his property. During dry years, access to canal water is cut off chronologically from newest to oldest rights. Properties with newer water rights can lose access to the canal water. Ditch riders ride four-wheelers along the canals monitoring use and issuing citations when owners don't abide by restrictions. By purchasing such old water rights, my Dad and stepmom have confidence that water will flow, even during dry times.

As we flew into Bozeman, Greg pointed out the Bridger Mountains from the airplane, the site of his formidable Bridger Ridge Run on Saturday. Our first night in MT, we went to Buffalo Jump Sports Bar and Gentleman's Club. We went to the sport's bar side of the establishment– safely sequestered from the nefarious other side. The bar is a mile from my parents' house, and they steadfastly refused to set foot on the premises for years – the Gentleman's Club side of the establishment was *not* their kind of folk. This past year, my stepmom went on a lengthy trip and my Dad eventually found the home kitchen unstocked. Normally he does the family cooking, but an injury impeded his usual shopping and cooking rhythm. In an act of desperation, he ventured down to the sports bar and walked into a warm, lively setting with good food, local beer, and bubbly, spunky staff. He and my stepmom now eat there regularly – five dollar spaghetti on Wednesdays and ½ price ribs on Fridays.

The kids and I woke up Saturday to a cool, arid Montana morning – where the day could start in the 40s and get up into the 80s by mid-day. Greg left around 4am to head to the race start at Fairy Lake. I thought about Greg all morning and kept looking at the mountains, imagining him running along the crest. I hoped he was feeling strong, enjoying the views out over the valley. We drove to the race finish around 1p. Greg thought he would take 6 or 7 hours to finish. The last couple of miles of the race are a steep descent past a large letter "M" made from white rocks on the mountainside and down to a gravel parking lot. The Bridger finish is a festive scene, with lots of cheering supporters, tired and sometimes bloody finishers, a food tent, and a medical tent.

Tired runners kept coming into boisterous cow bells and cheers. Most of the finishers had dirt crusted legs and big smiles. Just at the 7-hour mark, Greg appeared with another runner, high above us on the final descent. They jogged and scrambled their way down the rocky path. We all cheered loudly. I was so happy to see him come across the finish. He needed a few minutes to cool down and refuel. Greg almost always meets and makes friends during races and he met quite a few new folks during this run, including an amputee and another cancer survivor.

A story shared by another cancer survivor stays with me. Some cancer survivors believe that cutting sugar out of their diet will reduce their chance of cancer recurrence. After Greg's surgery, one of the nurse practitioners at Duke mentioned the ketogenic diet. The theory is that cancer cells suck down glucose to do their dirty deeds and that cutting out sugar starves cancer cells of their fuel. Non-cancer cells can use some of their inner workings to create energy from protein and fat. While the concept may hold up in theory, sustaining a ketogenic diet for any length of time is a great challenge. During a visit with her oncologist, the other runner, trying to cut out sugar, described talking about her wishes to have a piece of chocolate cake for her birthday. Her oncologist told her that she didn't spend months and months enduring difficult treatment to cure her cancer so that she could then skip her birthday cake out of fear. "Have a piece of cake on your birthday," he told her. Treating cancer isn't just to wipe cancer cells out of the body, but also to help the survivor continue to live for celebrations and pleasures.

A few days later, we said our good-byes in MT and loaded onto the airplane to head back home. After flying all day, we arrived home late Wednesday night to gifts of chocolate, wine, and a hand-painted card from my NC parents. Our friend Dawn had left a beautiful scrapbook of letters of support from Kona Inspired and photos from Angels Among Us.

Cold

Greg has written about being a cancer survivor. The word "survivor" carries strength, authority, gravity. Whether by war, abuse, abandonment, illness, or injury, a survivor has experienced hardship. Before July 2012, I considered a cancer survivor as somebody who was diagnosed with cancer in the past, has gone through treatment, and is cured or in remission. If somebody was not cured or in remission, then I considered them a cancer patient as opposed to a survivor. I now know that one becomes a cancer survivor at the moment of diagnosis and stays a survivor forevermore.

After Greg's last appointments, he took a step away from being a cancer patient and one step more solidly on the path of survivorship. Based on what we know now, Greg will be a cancer patient for the rest of his life. Today, though, this patient leaves chemotherapy behind. There are no monthly visits to the cancer pharmacy, no bi-monthly blood draws, no cancer-killing pharmaceuticals crossing the blood-brain barrier. There may be weeks when he is tired and cranky and has a grumbly tummy, but it won't be because he took chemo the night before.

Greg had an MRI, bloodwork, and urine test on Monday. We think the urine test was to measure kidney function for the PET scan the following day. Tuesday was the PET scan and meeting with neuro-oncologist. During this visit, the cancer center felt less forgiving, less personal than at his last appointments. I didn't connect with the warmth and familiarity I felt at his June appointments. I felt anxious, with a tinge of weariness. This time, I did not find comfort in the familiar faces, the other patients, the glowing gas flame on the back wall of the main entrance. Except for the urinalysis, Monday's tests were old hat for us. Tuesday held the gravity, with the PET scan and meeting with oncologists.

I could not be with Greg for his PET scan. After being administered the radioactive glucose, he must be completely still and quiet for an hour – no reading, talking, or listening to music. After the scan, Greg told me that the radioactive glucose administered through his IV came in a grapefruit sized cauldron with thick walls and a sticker warning of radiation.

After the PET scan, we went to check in at the Brain Tumor Center. The receptionist greeted us with a big smile and went to check Greg in. "Um, I don't see your appointment. Oh, wait, your appointment is for 8:45 tomorrow morning." Crap. We'd rescheduled Greg's appointments because initially they were scheduled for Belle's first day of school, which wouldn't work at all. During the rescheduling process, everything was bumped back a day, except, apparently, for the oncology apt. We waited a bit while the receptionist went to check in with the triage nurse. She came back and said that the doctor could see us in the afternoon.

Oh, the nerves. The angel and devil were back on my shoulders, whispering their sweet and sour musings. "The scan was fine, there are no active cancer cells, no surprises" said the angel. "Your last appointment was weird, the doctor sure is taking a while to come into the room, they found some active cells," the devil suggested. Tick, tock, tick, tock.

The PA came in for the usual neuro checks. "How are you?" she asks. Greg says, "Nervous." She says that she does not know the scan results. Greg counts backwards from 100 by 7s, touches his nose with his eyes closed, is asked to remember three words (the same three words as the last visit: apple, table, penny). Tick tock, tick tock. The neuro-oncologist comes in. I look at her face for any hints of the test results. She sits on the wide chair next to me, instead of the twirly stool by the computer. She never sits next to us. Why is she sitting in a different seat? She asks about Kona. She thinks Greg will try again next year, seems confused when he says "No, I won't try again." She says that next year he may be faster and stronger. We don't want to talk about Kona. "I'll give you the good news first," she says. That must mean there is bad news. What is the bad news? "Your MRI is stable. Your PET scan is cold. Your tests all look great, what we want to see. You can stop the chemo." What is the bad news?

There is no bad news. Greg is set "free" – no chemo, just watchful waiting. How crippled are the remaining cancer cells? He will continue to get MRIs every two months for the first year off treatment. He will continue to take anti-seizure medicine. If he is stable after this year, then he can get an EEG and possibly come off the anti-seizure medicine.

On July 11, 2012, Greg became a cancer survivor. He lay unconscious on an operating room table, his skull sawed open, his brain exposed. The neurosurgeon cut into his brain using MRI-guided robotic surgical techniques, removing an egg-sized mass from his right frontal lobe. A pathologist waited in the OR. The pathologist collected a tissue sample from the mass and looked at the cells. I assume a microscope was involved, but I don't know. Oligodendroglioma, possibly anaplastic. Either way, cancer. At that moment, Greg's identity changed. Survivor. At that moment, my identity changed. Caregiver, wife of a cancer patient. Except for marriage and childbirth, no other moment has affected my identity more than when my husband was diagnosed with incurable brain cancer. Parts of me have been shed like snakeskin. I leave behind security, stability, grantedness. The new me awaits – cool, exposed, glistening, ready to face the world.

September 14, 2013

"Look closer and closer, and look further and further,
and listen harder and harder to the noise of the earth and the
silence of the stars and what you will hear is a small voice
that whispers … Don't try to get, try to give."
~ Rob Ryan

900 Miles

Our story changes direction here. Two years pass between my last writing of updates for friends and family, and my next writing. Cancer is not always front and center. Greg gets an MRI every two months. The time surrounding the first few scans is filled with anxiety. Greg has a series of clean scans; we take a breath.

After Greg's Kona Inspired video received the highest number of views, we were crushed when he did not receive a spot at the Ironman World Championships in Hawaii. I seethed with anger for months, swearing to never, ever compete in any World Triathlon Federation event in my life. Greg was a master at making lemonade from lemons, at spinning gold from straw. He left Kona behind and jumped into what became known as "Quad B" or "Badousa Brain Bike Bonanza." Greg pulled ideas and energy from people he admired, specifically Terry Fox and Tony McEachern.

Terry Fox is a Canadian athlete whom Greg admired years before being diagnosed with cancer. Terry was diagnosed with osteosarcoma in 1977 at age 18, his leg amputated as part of treatment. In 1979, after training for 14 months, he started what he called the Marathon of Hope –a run across Canada to raise money for cancer research and awareness. He ran a marathon a day, every day, for 143 days on one good leg and one prosthetic. During the run, his cancer returned and he was forced to stop. He died on June 28th, 1981. Just prior to his death, he raised around $25-million dollars, reaching his goal of raising one dollar for every Canadian. His story is breathtaking – he was so young when he started his run. There are videos of him running along empty Canadian roads in the beating sun and in the pouring rain. He had a signature gait of a stride and a hop as he pulled his prosthetic along, mile after mile after mile. Terry's prosthetic looks like a dinosaur compared to what modern medicine has today. Terry's commitment to building his body from the wreckage of cancer treatment became a fire in Greg's belly.

Tony McEachern is another patient at Duke's Brain Tumor Center. He was diagnosed with anaplastic astrocytoma in 2002. After years of surgeries and treatments, he walked from Durham NC to his home in Sarasota FL to raise money for Duke's Brain Tumor Center. He raised $57,000 and went on to start the Team Tony Foundation, an organization that connects cancer survivors and caregivers with others on the cancer journey for one-on-one support. Soon after he was diagnosed, Greg connected with Tony.

After the Kona loss, Greg made plans to ride his bike from Durham, NC to Ormond Beach, FL where he would join in with Team Tony's 200-mile cycling fundraiser known as the "Team Tony Cycle of Life". Greg would pedal 700 miles down the east coast from Durham to Ormond Beach and then add 200 additional miles to Sarasota with Tony's ride. Greg's trip would cover 900 miles and take approximately two weeks.

Greg planned his trip efficiently and set off from Durham, NC on his bike on September 24, 2013. He left from the cancer center with a large celebration. Friends, family, staff from the cancer center, and a local news channel gathered with balloons and signs and music as he set off on his adventure. His friend Shawn biked with him the first two days of the trip and another friend, Branson, drove along as support. Greg then rode solo until reaching Jacksonville, FL where he met another friend. He met friends along the way, never having to pay for food or lodging.

He called home every night, sharing stories of the sights and sounds of the southeast coast. His most memorable moments were times where traffic was minimal, and nature's stillness filled his spirit and moved his legs along. Towards the end of his trip, the kids and I flew down to Florida for the Cycle of Life. We stayed at a hotel near the race finish, joining friends and family of other riders. Because his tumor affected balance and peripheral vision, Tony rides a tandem bike. The kids and I went to the finish to cheer Tony and Greg and hundreds of other riders. People payed special attention to the two brain tumor patients, dedicating every cell in their bodies to moving forward and to raising money and awareness for thriving with cancer. To this day, the Team Tony Foundation website has a picture of Tony and Greg biking together on this ride. Tony is on the back of a tandem bike, another rider in front. Greg's front wheel and Tony's back wheel are just a few inches apart. Tony reaches back, Greg reaches forward, hands briefly connected.

With an initial fund-raising goal of $10,000, Greg raised over $40,000 for the Brain Tumor Center. His ride was a success in every way possible. He navigated the physical and logistical challenges, he pushed his body farther than he ever had before, and he raised tens of thousands of dollars for cancer research. After the sting of losing Kona, he roared back, pedaling his way down the southeast coast from the cancer center to another cancer survivor.

A few months after his Florida trip, Greg had another grand mal seizure. He was home and fortunately, the kids were away and I was with him. I was moving furniture around in our study to make room for a piano, and heard what initially sounded like an odd sort of singing or grunting from the living room. After a few seconds, I poked my head in the living room to investigate. Greg lay on the floor, his back arched and legs bent. After a second or two of having no clue what was happening, I realized he was having a seizure. I rushed over, turned him to his side, put his head near me, and called 911. My cell phone reception was crummy and I ended up panicking and crying trying to talk to the operator. They dispatched emergency services.

Often, a seizure is not a medical emergency. Because of Greg's cancer history, the length of his seizure, and the extent of his confusion after the seizure stopped, the ambulance took him to the emergency department. He stabilized quickly and ended up coming home after just a few hours. His brain tumor doctors scheduled an MRI and saw him the next day. His MRI showed no new tumor growth. The worst physical damage was his shredded tongue that got mangled between his clenched, seizing teeth. The doctors increased his seizure medicine and attributed the seizure to a cold and fever he had earlier in the week. Our sense of calm was disrupted, but we felt better that the cancer had not returned. Greg was placed on driving restrictions again and I went back to being the family driver.

After one year of clean scans, Greg graduated to having an MRI every three months. At his first three-month scan, the oncologist noticed a small but new spot, popping up along the margin of his surgical cavity.

She switched Greg back to being scanned every two months, stating that the new spot could be scar tissue, but she wanted to keep an eye on it. It grew ever so slightly over the next couple of scans. After a few months of watching the spot, Greg's oncology team decided to do a biopsy. They still mentioned the possibility of post-surgical scar tissue.

For the biopsy, Greg wore a metal frame that literally screwed into his skull. A beautiful neurosurgery resident was the doctor responsible for screwing the cage onto Greg's scull, wiping drops of blood off with one hand as she twisted the screws into his bone with the other. As she stepped out of the room, Greg managed to make jokes about being screwed by another woman and made me laugh. Instead of sawing a window out of Greg's scull (and then replacing it), the surgeon drilled into the exact spot of the new growth and took a tiny core of tissue. The tissue went to pathology for analysis. After the biopsy came back as cancer, I started writing updates again, to keep our circle of support updated.

The Second Surgery, September 2015

Out Out Dern Spot!!

Greg's last MRI revealed new tumor growth. The September biopsy came back as cancer. He is scheduled for surgery to remove the tumor on Wednesday, September 23rd. His first day post op is exactly two years from the date he left on his bike ride to FL. He will be admitted to Duke Hospital and plans to be discharged home after three nights. He has the same neurosurgeon as before. After healing, he will move into another year of chemo.

Twas the Night Before . . .

. . . Surgery.

Greg is checked into the hospital and, last I heard, was prepped for his pre-surgery MRI. Hopefully he'll get a few zzz's before morning. He is first on deck with the surgeon, who is optimistic about surgery. He likes to schedule simpler surgeries first, leaving his afternoon spot for more difficult operations that could conceivably go hours into the night.

Yesterday, the kids took a class with the child life specialist to learn about what cancer is and how doctors treat it. The kids blew piles of bubbles to demonstrate dividing cancer cells. Then they scooped out bubbles like a surgery, pinched bubbles like chemotherapy, and used a straw to blow out bubbles like radiation (no radiation for Greg, just part of the learning). They also played with models of CT scans and MRI machines.

While at the cancer center, we saw a man in a bike helmet and safety vest playing the downstairs Steinway grand piano. His brown skin stood in contrast to the white, marble floor. His fingers moved with confidence, playing an unfamiliar tune. Based on attire, he looked to be a maintenance person at the cancer center, channeling the stress from his day into the wood and ivory of the grand piano. His story was clearly different from Greg's, but the bike helmet and reflective vest looked so much like Greg when he heads out on his bike in the morning. His music was complicated and strong, the kids were captivated.

Resting in Bed

Greg is out of surgery and resting in bed. His ICU room is in the newest hospital wing with the boring name of "Medical Pavilion." His room is spacious, bright, with gleaming towers of outlets, pumps, numerous places to hang IV bags, and monitoring equipment. The first thing his nurse said to me is, "Your husband was being pretty goofy when he first got up here." Phew, that means the surgery must have gone well.

He's waiting for the doctors to come in and remove a pressure bandage from his head. He's able to drink some ginger ale. His surgeon is not a man of many words and said, "Everything went well." Greg says he's most ready for the first week to be over. He remembers the first week being particularly hard after his first surgery.

Even though there is a place for me to sleep here, I'll be home with the kids this evening. The first surgery I stayed at the hospital, but since we've been through this before, we're trying to maximize stability for Belle and Abe.

Going Home

They are discharging Greg home today, a day early. So long as surgery goes well, with no complications, brain surgery patients do better at home than in the hospital. They're getting the discharge paperwork ready now.

That Awkward Moment When . . .

... the staff discharging you from the neuro ICU smiles and says, "Come back and see us sometime!"

After a hurried and somewhat unexpected discharge from the hospital this morning, Greg is resting at home. We set up a recliner chair in the living room and he is kicked-back resting. Papi is off getting us lunch and Greg's discharge meds while I wash our bed linens.

We are grateful that there were no complications at the hospital and Greg can be with us at home to begin the healing process.

That Other Awkward Moment When . . .

... you realize you completely forgot that your mother-in-law was having her 9th round of chemo for her breast cancer (because you were schlepping her son home from the hospital for his brain cancer). Greg and his mom could have taken cancer naps together yesterday.

Today, Greg is doing well. He is stiff and sore. It is a wet, rainy day and he's asked to go to the mall to do a bit of walking to stretch out his legs. We'll head over there for a bit and he can get in some walking and scare others at the mall (or else they'll think he's really on the ball for his Frankenstein Halloween costume).

Up and at Em

Greg is doing great. Sleep is restless, but that has been his rhythm after the last surgery and biopsy, so he is somewhat mentally prepared. He's only on the steroids for a few days. Once he comes off those, sleep gets better. We undressed his wound this morning, winding yards of thin, white gauze down to his olive skin. He has a long line of stitches following the same scar as the first surgery – small lines of sturdy, black thread with tiny knots caked in dried blood. We learned that the surgeon cuts along the old scar; otherwise, there is a risk of more serious tissue damage.

Greg feels no cognitive change from before surgery, which is a huge victory. He feels (and acts) lucid and coordinated. His first few post-op appointments are set up – one to remove stitches and a pre-treatment appointment for chemo.

Rainy Weekend

The weekend has gone surprisingly well. Greg's biggest bumps are a mixed-up sleep cycle (lots of daytime naps, up at night) and quite sore muscles in his back and hamstrings. He got up this morning and made pancakes – a wholesome mix of whole wheat flour, ground flax, and a handful of dark chocolate chips.

Unstitched

Big Man got all 77 stitches out today. It was a mental and physical milestone for him. He says that the staples after his first surgery were more difficult. For the staples, it took a couple of appointments and several nurses. All his stitches came out in one visit. No shower for a couple of days and no swimming/bathing/water immersion for several weeks. His scar is poufy, a river of tender flesh across the top of his head – we'll have to see how it recedes with time.

One night this past week, Belle woke up after midnight complaining of stomach pain. This is unusual for her. No fever or other symptoms, just stomach pain. Greg was downstairs being an insomniac, so I invited her into our bed where I could rub her back and hopefully help her feel better. Greg then came back into bed. All four of us ended up crashing (Abe still in his room) until after 7am. Belle's tummy felt better and we had a mad scramble to get to school on time (only a few minutes late).

Blazeman (Part One)

As a youth, Greg rode BMX – trick riding and motocross. Not having a driver's license meant needing a parent willing to drive him around to races. Greg connected with another rider named Jon Blais (pronounced "Blaze"). Their dads took turns driving the boys to BMX racetracks. Greg and Jon weren't close friends, but kept each other company during drives to races. Both guys grew up and then away from New England, not staying in touch.

As an adult, Greg's athletic pursuits drifted away from BMX and into triathlons and its component pieces. He went on to compete in many triathlons and several Ironman events. While watching the 2005 Hawaii Ironman Championships on TV, the name of a participant tickled his memory. Jon Blais.

His body already affected by the disease, Jon received recognition for being the first-ever ALS survivor to complete Hawaii Ironman. He finished the race in just over 16 hours. Jon died within two years of finishing the race. After connecting the dots between himself and Jon via BMX, during one of his trips home to RI, Greg stopped to visit and talk with Jon's parents.

Today is the 10-year anniversary of Jon's Hawaii Ironman completion. His friends and family now run The Blazeman Foundation for ALS. We've had live coverage of the 2015 Hawaii Ironman streaming on our computer all day, rain clinking down on our skylights. I still hold bitterness about the unfolding of Kona Inspired. However, I am also reminded of Jon's focus and intensity when he competed in 2005 and the willpower and determination of each athlete starting the race today. The human body is brilliant. Even when disease takes hold, our spirits dig deep and pull our bones, muscles, and hearts along, reminding others of all that we are capable of.

We Got the Brandermill Blues

Today Greg had his "pre-treatment" appointment at the cancer center. Belle woke up with a fever and malaise and our car key did not work in the ignition. We did some begging and shuffling and got our bases covered. We borrowed our neighbor's car and my dad stayed with Belle while Greg and I took Abe to school and then went to his appointment.

After initial bloodwork, Greg's oncology team gave him the green light to start chemo today. He met with the mid-level provider to discuss his chemo schedule and logistics, and do the usual neuro checks. Two years having passed since his last pills, he opted to do the chemo teaching session again – meeting with a nurse to go over precautions and side effects. Greg will take nausea medicine during his chemo cycle and over-the-counter "keep the pipes moving along" meds.

We headed down to the pharmacy to pick up his chemo and learned that he still needed prior authorization from insurance, which can take a day or two. Having been through this process before, we weren't overly flustered. We left the clinic with plans to come back, possibly tomorrow, to pick up his chemo.

Round Two, Cycle One

I debated the title of this section. Should it be Cycle Thirteen? Cycle Two, Round One? The title of my writing from his last chemo was called "Cycle Twelve". Whatever the title, here Greg is at the doorstep of another round of chemo.

I'm feeling blue at the moment. I learned earlier today that a friend's husband's lymphoma returned, soon after a long and difficult stretch of very aggressive treatment. They have two young children. I very much hoped that his cancer would stay away.

So, tonight Greg will take the nausea medicine and three pills of cancer killer. I am grateful that he has this treatment option, that he can take his meds at home and be relatively functional, and that he is able to be strong and positive.

Bozeman Comes to Bull City

This week, my Dad and stepmom, aka Grandpa and Gramona, came to visit from Bozeman, MT. Our time together went well, although a little hectic. Our weeks are busy with school, work, and the kids' activities.

Greg continues to rebound from surgery. The first round of chemo sapped some of his energy and helped with some of his insomnia problems. Some of the other creaks and bumps in his body are working their way out. He's been walking and jogging a bit and has been out on his bikes for short rides.

Over the next year, he'll have to figure out the flow of all of his monthly bloodwork appointments. He has a new job in a different location, which means he'll likely end up going to Duke's cancer center for bloodwork and then scooting into work. He's learning the feel of precise and not-so-precise phlebotomists.

Blazeman (Part Two)

In January 2015, Greg read an article in a local sports magazine about a woman named Andrea with ALS who was competing in a Ramblin' Rose triathlon. Pieces of her story stood out to him – the tenacity of doing a triathlon with ALS and the story of her favorite number, 179. 179 became her lucky number in middle school when she played a Holton Farkas French horn, model 179. Years later, before being diagnosed with ALS, she learned of John Blais who wore bib number 179 when he became the first person with ALS to complete Ironman Hawaii. In 2013, after experiencing muscle weakness and pain, Andrea was diagnosed with ALS.

Greg outreached to Andrea to connect on the spirit of competing in athletic events after a life-changing medical diagnosis. They talked on the phone and connected via e-mail and social media. Greg learned of Andrea's plans to enter Raleigh's City of Oaks Marathon as a fundraiser for Jon Blais' Blazeman Foundation. She would compete in a special bike designed for her. Greg and a few coworkers signed on to be part of a relay team supporting Andrea's cause.

Springtime came and went, the City of Oaks Marathon relay sat on our calendar as a fun, future charity event. Then Greg's cancer returned. The relay was scheduled 5 weeks after surgery. Greg pulled from his memory of his first surgery and knew he had a good chance of being able to complete the 6-mile portion of his relay. He often spoke of the difference between "compete" and "complete".

This past Saturday, the four Sousas piled in our car and headed to a luncheon for the people supporting Andrea's City of Oaks race. Greg and Andrea coordinated with Jon Blais' parents to have some of Jon's ashes sent to Andrea. Jon asked that after he died, his ashes be scattered in beautiful places he would not be able to visit. Andrea asked if Greg would speak at the luncheon, before she scattered Jon's ashes along the shore of Lake Johnson. Surrounded by Andrea and her friends and family, Greg gave a moving testament to Andrea and to Jon. Thirty years separated two boys sharing car rides to BMX races to one spreading the ashes of the other along the sandy edge of a wooded lake. Below is a quote from Andrea that captures her spirit:

"Walking through the finish chute with everyone cheering and crying, honestly, I couldn't look around. I would have lost it. People say I inspired then, but it is nothing compared to what reverberated through me from all sides. It was the very best of humanity. What is it like to have that force of compassion directed at you? It defies words. Jon Blais knew. And now I know too. All I can say is thank you to all the members of the newly expanded Team Drea. Thank you for creating a memory and an emotion that my friends, family, and I will never, ever forget."

We left the luncheon to head into an evening of Halloween activities.

Greg woke up early Sunday morning for the race, hitching a ride with his relay team. I dropped the kids off with my parents and then headed to Raleigh to meet Greg and others. I was lucky enough to be able to meet up with Andrea's parents at the finish line. A warm rain came in and we stood in anticipation, waiting for Andrea to come across the finish line. After about 4½ hours, Andrea came pedaling in, surrounded by her team of supporters. There were lots of cheers and smiles – it is humbling and gratifying to be present when somebody accomplishes a goal born from a deep and profound ache. The frivolity of malls and gas stations and dusty floors slips behind the beauty of calling somebody friend, of saying "I love you", of paying witness to the raw grit of sweaty, tired people hugging behind a finish line.

Zip Lining and Gem Mining

This past weekend was our annual trip to Asheville for the Shut-In Ridge trail run. Or, as Greg's oncologist called it at his last appointment, the "Shit-In Run??" That was a funny visit.

After running 11 years in a row, this year Greg did not run, instead volunteering with the legendary Bob Cutler at HW 151. This is at mile 16 of the 18-mile course, also known as the 1/2-way point. The ascent from 151 to the finish is as brutal as the first 16 miles. Bob is now 82 years old. His last running of the race, also his 25th consecutive race, was in 2004 at Greg's first time at the race. Bob was a sprightly 71 years old at the time.

The kids had Friday off school, so we drove up Thursday evening. We stay at a hotel, bingeing on cable TV and the breakfast waffle machine. With a friend's suggestion, we found a place to zipline. They have a special course for kids under 10 years old. We paid way too much money and had an absolute blast – flinging our harnessed bodies along a winding cable strung 15 feet above a grassy field. Greg has wanted to take the kids ziplining for a while, but our featherweight kiddos didn't hit the minimum weight requirement. For this course, the kids went through the 9-zip course at least 10 times and would have kept going.

Saturday morning, Greg headed up the mountain with other racers and volunteers. The day was cool and rainy, so the kids and I decided to not venture over to the race site. We mostly left cancer worries behind. Greg wasn't able to run because of his surgery, but enjoyed the change of pace and action with volunteering.

Calm, Cycle Two

Greg finished his 2nd round of chemo yesterday. He held strong and showed little sign of wear and tear. He gets tired conks out in the evening, but perseveres to get through the mechanics of the day.

Today we ran with our local running club at an event called the Misery Run. It was definitively not miserable. The kids went with my parents to church and Greg and I had the morning together. The 5.7-mile event was his longest trail run since surgery. The race involves running through fields and root strewn trails, jumping over hay bales, and tromping through enormous piles of cow-poo (as in chest deep). At the beginning of the run, the race director says that any participants who are immunocompromised should not do the event. Greg ignores this advice – the race director explained that it's possible to get one's face in cow poo during the event. Greg wasn't particularly worried about this possibility.

Threads

Greg pulls strength from people like Terry Fox and Billy Mills. Billy Mills is a Native American who won a gold medal in the 1964 Tokyo Olympics in the 10,000-meter run. At the end of a long day, Greg sometimes sits at the computer, watching Billy's electric, come-from-behind finish. Through his own feats of athleticism and optimism after surgery and treatment, Greg provides strength to others.

As Greg has lived with cancer, going through two surgeries and into his second year of chemo, we've connected with others whose journeys remind us of hardship, gratitude, and blessings. During our recent trip to Asheville, we learned that a fellow brain tumor patient had a setback resulting in a car accident. A few weeks later, Greg was biking with a friend on a trail near our house. He saw this fellow patient out for a run, also with a friend. The other brain tumor patient slowed to a stop, telling his friend, "wait, wait, I need to stop and say hi to this guy." The two chatted briefly. To others on the trail, the scene was just two friends stopping to talk during a morning workout. Underneath the surface, it was two brain tumor patients connecting along the difficult journey of cancer and the unsettling and unexpected surprises that can take our planned lives off course.

Sunday Ride

Greg raced at the Raleigh BMX track today, Capital City BMX. It was his first race since surgery. He's wanted to ride for a few weeks, but weather and holidays kept him away. This was a big mental break for him – pushing himself on the track after the beating of a craniotomy. His big-bad-self came in first place! He'll lay low in the BMX race world for a bit now. The track quiets down during the winter. He'll still do some ramp and trick riding and keep up his runs and bike commuting.

Our Christmas tree us up and we've had the woodstove going. A new season is upon us.

Stars

I am not a night person. If I'm lucky, the kids are in bed by 8p and I'm in bed by 9p. I'm not lucky very often. If I'm not in bed, then I'm running on fumes once the clock hits 9pm. I'm usually awake between 5a and 5:30a, refreshed and ready to tackle the day.

Several mornings a week, I meet my friend Vicky to run at 5:30a. During the summer, we're just getting the first light of day. In the winter, it is often pitch black as we head out. I step out of my warm, quiet house and the cold winter air makes my ears burn. As I walk down the street, I look up and see the sky full of stars – not just the few pinpricks of light that started out the evening before, but a full and dazzling blanket of all the winter constellations. I am overwhelmed by the powerful reminder of how tiny we are. My fingers tingle and my core wells with awe as I remember that our planet is a mere dot in the vast and unimaginable expanse of space and energy and stars and light and matter and asteroids and mystery. Whatever I got going on is nothing. Really, it's completely, absolutely nothing. Then, I see my friend and I am grateful for her company. Our legs carry us through the neighborhood and we talk about kids and school and work and NPR and my world shifts back to being front and center.

The Sunday after Thanksgiving, I saw Christmas lights hung around the neighborhood and struggled with not feeling confused. How the heck could it be Christmas already – school had just started, right? It really didn't make sense; I'd definitely not transitioned into the Christmas season, yet. Greg and I went to Belle and Abe's school for Friday Morning Prayer. The program was a festive spin on Advent. A middle school class explained the meaning of Advent – a time to prepare for the arrival of Jesus. We sang and watched a funny music video about Advent set to the tune of "Gangnam Style." The Principal talked about how every class participated in a service project to provide lunches to over 300 people at the homeless shelter. Surrounded by children and music and reminders of our call to generosity, I was finally ready for the Christmas Spirit.

This past Sunday, Belle and Abe were in the Pilgrim Christmas Pageant – Belle played a surly Innkeeper and Abe was more welcoming to the out-of-town guests. Mary and Joseph successfully navigated their way through the twists and turns of poor lodging options and found their way to the manger.

Now, it is 11 days until Christmas and I am happily surrounded by the story of Christ's birth. Reading the Christmas story as factual feels creepy and weird to me – nothing about the virgin birth makes sense. When I read the story as a fairy tale from God, then its message slides into my soul and fills me with wonder and hope and appreciation for how much goodness us humans are capable of. The story reminds me of the power of love between a husband and wife under untenable circumstances, of the painful and centering journey of pregnancy, of angels who guide and comfort us when we are overwhelmed with questions, of Christ's power to connect to all walks of life, of dreams that nudge us away from bad decisions, of a star that extracts itself from the tangle of its other companions to lead magi to the feet of a humble, exhausted family. Baby Jesus lies in a manger, unknowingly on the precipice of changing the world and reminding humanity of our call to feed, clothe, and care for the humble and the hurt.

First Scan Since Surgery

On Wednesday, Greg had his first scan since surgery. We clicked into our usual routine for his appointments at the cancer center involving an MRI and oncology meeting. He woke up early and headed out on his bike before 6a. I got the kids up and off to school and then met Greg. Earlier in treatment, I tried to make it to his MRIs. After more than a dozen scans, we realized that logistically, it made sense for him to do the scan alone and I could meet him for the oncology apt.

His appointment went well. He saw a new nurse practitioner whom we both really liked – she was energetic, engaging, and had a great bedside manner. She started the appointment by saying, "your scan looks great." The appointment goes so much better when we get the feedback on Greg's scan right away – that's the biggest, most important news. She then asked questions about how he is doing and what side effects he was having from chemotherapy. Once the outcome of the scan is covered, then the flow of the appointment is routine.

Duke's Brain Tumor Center focuses on maximizing quality of life for as long as possible. The medical team has a toolbox full of treatment options – surgery, genetic analysis of tumor type, an array of chemotherapies, immunotherapies, protein therapies, radiation, and lifestyle choices like exercise. They carefully consider each tool in the toolbox and balance what will stop the cancer with what effect that will have on the patient's quality of life. They love Greg – he embodies their mission of approaching brain tumors with hope and of being able to live a full, active life after diagnosis, with minimal impact on quality of life. His providers gush with accolades: *"The resection looks wonderful, the margins are beautiful!" "Wow, you can hardly even see your scar, your hair covers it right up!" "You biked here, that's just fantastic! It's fabulous that you're so active!" "You're not having many side effects from the chemo? That's just great!"*

All of these statements are true and we are immensely grateful for where Greg is after two surgeries and into a second year of treatment. The combination of the skills of his medical team, the nature of his cancer, and his attitude and perseverance make him a poster child for the successes of modern medicine.

Still, the energy of his appointment leaves me dissatisfied. The tone of the medical teams' gushing over their and Greg's accomplishments were indistinguishable from accolades one might hear when announcing a pregnancy, celebrating a child's graduation, or sharing plans for an upcoming trip to Spain. The seriousness and weight of looking at an MRI showing a large cavity of missing brain and discussing optimal chemotherapy dosing for cancer treatment was tucked away for Greg and me to grapple with later.

The appointment ended with Greg's oncologist deciding to increase his chemotherapy dosing and keeping his twice monthly bloodwork checks (there was talk of moving to once a month). During his first round of chemotherapy in 2012/2013, the doctors adjusted his dose based on bloodwork. This time, they started him out on the lower, entry dose. His bloodwork looks great, so the oncologist wants to go up to what she called optimal dosing. They'll continue to keep an eye on symptoms and blood counts. His 5-nights of chemo will be finished by Sunday, well before Christmas.

Holiday 2015

Greg finished his 3rd round of chemo the Sunday before Christmas. He noticed the higher dose of medicine, mainly in his digestive system. He works to balance the gut-locking effects of chemo with the biological need to keep things moving. The balance was difficult this time around and he felt lackluster about certain food choices. His tiredness carried out a few more days than before. He fell biking on a local pump track and ended up with a bloody knee and bruised ribs, disrupting sleep.

Greg's parents visited again for Christmas this year. Last year, I felt grumpy during the holiday preparation time. I was annoyed and frustrated pulling boxes out of the attic and having to move around clutter to make room for a Christmas tree. This year, I felt more relaxed and appreciative. I loved having Greg's parents visit – we missed a fall visit when his Mom was in treatment for breast cancer. His parents slide easily into our routine and the physical space of our home. His mom sits and works on crochet blankets and hats – sitting among bundles and rows of brightly colored yarn. His dad sweeps leaves in the front yard and tells the kids stories about growing up on a dairy farm – his version of walking to school in the snow uphill both ways. They go out for coffee each morning and bring the kids back doughnuts.

Since Christmas, we've had more interaction with our healthcare system than we'd like. Abe ran full force into a hard block at gymnastics camp and suffered testicular trauma. I took him to urgent care and the doctor took one look and sent us to the pediatric ED at Duke for a urology consult. After a very lengthy ultrasound, he was pronounced bruised but fine. Belle has had an on-again, off-again cold since Halloween. She was on a 10-day round of antibiotics before Christmas and ended with a head-to-toe rash. Her symptoms returned and today she tested positive for strep. She's on a new round of antibiotics (she says the pink elixir tastes like bug guts) and we're hopeful that she's done with germs for a while. I need to schedule routine eye and teeth exams, but put those off for all of the time and energy spent on the other health bumps that have headed our way.

Before Four

After a strangely balmy Christmas, winter is now here. The sharpness of cold air bites the backs of our throats as we step out in the morning. The woodstove has burned steady and hot for the last couple of weeks, the ash bucket filling every two to three days. We've also had a couple of hot chocolate nights. The stove is a lot of work, but the physical and emotional warmth that comes from a wood fire is worth it. Greg does all the manual labor around harvesting firewood. He scouts out fallen trees, transports rounds home, chops them for burning, and stacks pieces to dry. Once it's home and dried and winter has come, then he and I take turns starting a fire. His cancer treatment is a barrier to the time and energy needed to maintain enough firewood for the whole winter. There are more weeks when he is busy with or tired from treatment. For now, our firewood stack is high and we are warm.

He's seemed more tired this go-around (he's also been battling a cold). He is ready for bed early, falls asleep quickly, and works a little harder to get going in the morning. Fitting in exercise is challenging.

I often sit with the emotional weight that comes with a close family member with cancer. The scare of diagnosis, the battle wounds from surgery, the mental energy of coordinating appointments and trying to understand treatment plans, and the cloud of recurrence. Brain cancer feels unique in its chiseling at the essence of the survivor's identity and function.

I wish I could find some lightness and humor in Greg's cancer. Lightness and humor are at the core of Greg's identity. He knows that he has had a successful day when he makes me smile and laugh. If I'm stewing and brewing over something, he often breaks the mood by reminding me of lightness and relief hovering around the edges. He pulls those edges into me and helps me change my focus. We definitely have moments of laughter, but they are about the regular trials and tribulations of life. I just can't find much humor or even release in his cancer experiences. So, with Greg by my side, I will look for laughter in other places.

Tribe

I wonder how our lives would be different if Greg hadn't been diagnosed with brain cancer. I expect much would be surprisingly the same – our marriage is strong, Belle and Abe are glorious blessings, our house is warm and filled with love. These anchors have remained intact through the ups and downs of cancer. Greg and I have made professional decisions over the past 4 years that are related to his cancer diagnosis. He switched jobs and I made changes to my work hours which led to a change in my role at work (increased hours, increased responsibility). Greg and I work hard at our career/family balance – cancer has changed this dynamic some. Greg shifted from triathlons to BMX – the latter is an activity that he can do with the kids by his side.

Between planning meals and organizing medical appointments, I think about our tribe. I think about coming home from work and finding a 6-pack of beer, 2 chocolate bars, and lavender bath salts tucked in a paper bag on our porch. I think about dropping the kiddos off with my parents and meeting a dear friend for coffee while Greg chops firewood. Greg and I are continually blown away by the volume of love pouring our way. Our fridge and freezer are filled with stews delivered by neighbors and coworkers. My parents in Montana shipped us a cooler of frozen beef, elk, and lamb. My Montana parents and my aunt and uncle in Michigan sent us weeks of gift certificates for a local market that prepares take-and-bake scratch meals. We generally do well with one car, but during the times we want to be two different places at the same time, friends and family are eager to offer a ride or let us borrow a car. My parents live close and are always willing to help with the kids.

Receiving so much love and support inspires us to want to give back. We are each involved in local cancer support organizations – the Tisch Brain Tumor Center (Angels Among Us) and Cornucopia Cancer Support Center. When we can, we try to jump in and help others. This weekend we were snowed in by winter storm Jonas. Our neighborhood is alive with sleds and laughter and hot cocoa and smoking chimneys. Greg is comfortable driving in the snow and helped neighbors with a couple of small errands. He also mediated a group of tween boys who were being overly aggressive with their snowballs. I used my nursing skills for a couple of sledding accidents (nose versus rock and cheek versus back-of-head). No stitches or trips to urgent care were needed. Being in the south, the snow will soon melt and we'll be back to our regular day-to-day routine.

On Wednesday, Greg goes in for bloodwork. Even with winter settling in, he's biked to his past few oncology appointments in the cold, dark morning. Biking to the cancer center hits his checkbox on the side of life and strength. Greg's platelets took too much of a hit on the higher dose of chemo, so his oncologist dropped him back down to the lower dose. He'll stay at the lower dose for the rest of the year. We are grateful that his medical team keeps a close eye on him, balancing treatment and side effects. With all of his running, bike commuting, and BMX-ing he definitely needs his platelets.

The Third Surgery, February 2016

Placeholder

This is a super quick message, with more to follow. Greg is scheduled for surgery Friday. We were very surprised at the news – he's so soon out of his last surgery and had been on chemo. Cancer is sneaky.

More to follow . . .

The Cycle that Wasn't

This was supposed to be an update about Greg's 5th chemo cycle. Instead, it is about an unexpected turn. His MRI on February 10th showed a mass that has grown since his December scan. The mass isn't terribly big, but it is already bigger than the mass they removed in September.

The visit started off in a fairly regular and cheery manner. "Your blood counts look great!" "You're not having any symptoms, great!" "You tolerated that last cycle of chemo without major side effects, great!" Then we hear, "So, your scan shows new tumor growth. Let me show you."

This news is unexpected and we're confused. The oncologist pulls up Greg's scan and we can see the area of concern. We both silently wonder if there is a mistake.

The oncologist says there are a couple of options, but all paths lead to ending his current chemo regimen and starting a chemo/radiation combo. The question is whether or not Greg should have surgery. She has a call into the surgeon and is waiting to hear back. She says what we've heard before. It's better to start treatment, "with a clean slate." I ask about a biopsy instead of surgery. His oncologist says that if the biopsy shows a high-grade tumor, they'd have to take it out anyways, so they might as well go ahead and take it out. This is what they told us before Greg's first and second surgeries. We wait to hear from the surgeon. She plans for us to sit in on an education session with one of the clinic's nurse practitioners to get some initial education on radiation.

We move to a consult room to discuss patient information on the radiation/chemo combo. The conversation feels bizarre and unsettling. The nurse explains how Greg will take a low dose of oral chemo one hour before radiation (the same chemo he was on before, serving a different purpose). The chemo makes the tumor cells more vulnerable to the radiation. There will be appointments with the radiologist and fittings for a special mask. She goes over ins-and-outs of scheduling. She rattles off a bunch of potential side effects. Okey-dokey then.

No follow-up appointments are scheduled. We head off to lunch and process the morning. We touch base with family members.

Thursday, Greg gets a call asking if he can come into pre-op that day for surgery the following day. He hasn't even talked to his boss yet. That phone call is the only feedback we get that he should proceed with surgery. Greg goes through a couple of fits and starts with scheduling surgery. We have a few unanswered questions. The surgeon's schedule fills up. Finally, Greg and the neurosurgery team settle on a consult with the surgeon followed by surgery three days later.

In pondering the Brain Tumor Center's "hope" motto, I find myself drifting to a quote I read after Greg was diagnosed with cancer. A book club I'm in read Ann Patchett's novel *State of Wonder* (2011, Harper) . She writes, "Hope is a terrible thing, you know. I don't know who decided to package hope as a virtue because it's not. It's a plague. Hope is like walking around with a fishhook in your mouth and somebody keeps pulling it and pulling it."

The weekend is busy. We go see Deadpool Friday night. Awesome movie. Skip it if you don't like sex, foul language, and violence. Otherwise, it's tons of fun. The somewhat misguided hero gets his superpowers from cancer treatment gone awry. Greg and I run a 5K together (charity run for Cornucopia Cancer Support Center). We take Belle to a gymnastics meet in Greensboro, cheering loudly as she powers her muscles through the four events. Saturday evening, we tell the kids that it looks like Greg's cancer is growing again and the doctors need to come up with a new treatment plan. We don't mention surgery. Greg runs in a small, local trail run Sunday morning. We attend a charity event to support Cornucopia Sunday afternoon. We carry the weight of Greg's recurrence and go about our business.

Tuesday ends up being a flurry of appointments. We talk with Greg's surgeon. For him, the surgery is simple. The tumor "isn't very big" and it isn't compromising any critical brain structures. I suddenly understand what felt like a disconnect between oncology and surgery. They come at the same problem from two different perspectives. Greg's recurrence is of notable oncologic concern – unexpected growth while undergoing chemo. The tumor itself isn't much of a surgical concern – it's a mass that shouldn't be there, but the surgeon has tackled bigger and badder ones before.

We talked with nurses, the child life specialist, and a provider who works in cognitive testing. The team will assess his function as he moves through treatment. The vibe of the day is, "This sucks, but We. Got. This." The confidence and positivity of the team is contagious. We feel a bit more optimistic.

So, tomorrow Greg goes to pre-op and checks into the hospital. I'll take care of the kiddos (we told them about surgery) and meet up with Greg at the hospital Friday morning.

The weight of churning through the medical-industrial complex sits heavy. I feel terrible for Greg. Three craniotomies and one biopsy is a lot, even for a strong, young athlete. I see how much he hurts afterwards. The post-op steroids suck. The wound is tender. His head is budging and swollen. His mental energy is sapped from the grueling procedure and from the seriousness of a cancer diagnosis. Belle and Abe are anxious. Still, he hunkers down and gets through it. He sets physical goals – sleeping (much more difficult than you might think), walking, and, after a few weeks, jogging a lap at a woodsy loop near the hospital. He turns inward. He tells us how much he loves us. He fights. He fights hard.

Surgery Went Well

Greg is out of surgery and the neurosurgeon says everything went well. He'll rest today and hopefully go home soon. We'll await final pathology, but initial results show same tumor type, which is good. A more aggressive type would be worse news.

Greg will heal for 2 - 3 weeks and then move into his next phase of treatment.

Resting

Greg is doing well – eating, talking, making jokes. The beds are full at the hospital, so he'll stay in the PACU tonight. He has a side room with a sliding door that closes. Based on past experiences, I expect him to come home tomorrow.

Back on Brandermill

Greg's head is swollen and he has a gauze bandage over his wound, white threads standing in contrast to his black hair already beginning to grow in. Deep blue and purple hues settle in the soft skin under his eyes, just as in his past surgeries. The first surgery he had staples and the second stitches. This time, they went back to staples. Greg preferred the stitches – they are less jarring than staples upon removal. This counts for a lot when you have 70+ of them. Alas, he was under anesthesia at game time and didn't have an opportunity to express his preference.

I am happy he is home. I am happy that surgery went well and that all systems are working. I'm also sad and angry. Sad to see him have to go through another surgery. A craniotomy is rough. Cancer is rough. This journey has tapped us, sapped, us, and zapped us. Everything is shifted. While some blessings shine through, the overall path is rocky.

Strong

Our Gregory is so very strong. As worries of cancer cells consume my thoughts and deepen the creases of my furrowed brow, he pulls his golden-pedaled, lime green BMX bike out of the shed, pumps up the tires, and plans his next ride at the pump track a mile down the bike trail behind out house.

Considering what he went through on Friday, Greg is doing well. He's getting a few hours of sleep at night and hasn't needed pain medicine. Today, we went for a walk together and then out to lunch. We carry the exhaustion of his treatments and of the road ahead. Even so, he is full of determination – ready to plan for upcoming athletic events and ways to support the bigger cause of cancer survivorship.

Pissing the Night Away

Poor Greg has taken a downward turn. He looks, talks, and acts more like you would expect somebody to look, talk, and act after their third craniotomy (or, "cranie" as they said in the PACU). He's sore, tired, and not sleeping well. His back and legs hurt. His stomach is upset. His swelling has returned a bit. The on-call neurosurgery resident said something along the lines of, "take two zofran and call if things get worse." Greg is hobbling about, clearly fairly miserable.

I keep thinking of the Chumbawamba song "Tubthumping"

I get knocked down
But I get up again
You're never gonna keep me down
I get knocked down
But I get up again
You're never gonna keep me down
Pissing the night away
Pissing the night away

Our Dear Greg is ready for a new soundtrack. Stay tuned.

Stapled, Moldy, and Rolling

Greg is slowly climbing out of the "cranie" hole. Night brings a few hours of rest. It is a victory if he gets to bed by 9p and sleeps past midnight. From midnight until 6a he bounces around the house in various locations – downstairs couch, recliner chair, Abe's bed (if Abe has found his way to our bed, which happens more nights than not).

This morning, he left a note on the kitchen counter reading, "Can I cook us breakfast?" Why yes, of course! Greg cooked up a lovely breakfast. I sprinkled shredded cheese across the top and sat down to a plate of polenta, eggs, and bacon. My first bite revealed that the cheese had gone bad, giving everything a moldy taste. I promptly started crying. Greg retrieved my plate, managed to separate the rotten cheese from the eggs, gave me a 2nd helping of cheese-free polenta, and I tried again. My tears dried up and breakfast was saved.

When Greg was discharged from the hospital, the instructions said that his staples could come out on 7 - 10 days. We went to the clinic on

Friday in hopes of staple removal. Turns out that because he's had several incisions along the same line, the wound needs extra time to heal. The neurosurgery nurse suggests waiting 14 days before staple removal. So, he gets to look like Frankenstein a bit longer.

Today, Greg felt ready to try an easy bike ride. The first test was his helmet, which fit fine over his protective head wrap. Our friend Branson came over to ride along with Greg – a short bike ride along the American Tobacco Trail to a new pedestrian bridge that arcs over the interstate. Greg talked about likely needing to walk up the hill on the way home. Branson laughed and said something along the lines of, "Man, you biked to Florida, you won't need to walk!"

Late Friday afternoon, Greg got a call saying that he has an appointment with the radiation oncologist Monday morning. This will be a teaching and planning meeting. The next phase of treatment is likely to begin in about 10 days.

Rad Planning

Greg had an introductory, planning meeting with his radiation oncology team. If I wrote honestly, then my words would be a bitch session. Most of the morning I wanted to scream, cry, or throw-up. Our experience would have been GREATLY enhanced by a nurse or patient navigator helping coordinate the flow and organization of appointments and then sharing that information with us. 'Nuf said.

The good news is that we like his radiation oncology team. Like the script of a televised medical drama, they are young, confident, and paid attention during their one or two lectures on bedside manners in med school. They explained the process of radiation treatment. The next steps include a CT scan (Thursday) and an MRI (Friday). The team uses that information to create a custom mask that Greg will wear during treatment. This mask locks over Greg's face onto a table and helps ensure that his head will be in the exact same position for every treatment. Radiation is administered to the space along the inside of the surgical cavity, zapping the DNA of tumor cells. Radiation dosage is adjusted according to brain anatomy. The most common side effect is fatigue, plus whatever extra goodness comes from daily chemo (we'll get that info next week). The team says that exercise is a great antidote to the fatigue. Greg should be able to do as much of his usual routine as possible – eating, working, biking, driving, etc. He will check in with his radiation team at least once a week. He can get in touch with them at any point during his treatment, as needed. Each radiation session takes about 30 minutes. He'll go Monday through Friday for six weeks.

By the end of the day, Belle and Abe managed to bring a smile to my face. Belle offered a multitude of compliments about our evening meal (which doesn't happen so very often). Even though the meal was delivered by neighbors from Whole Foods, I took her compliments to heart. Abe has a little cold right now. I took him to pick up a new pair of school shoes and he was singing along with the radio on the way home. His cute little stuffy-nosed self was singing along to the 21 Pilots song "Stressed Out."

Wish we could turn back time, to the good ol' days,
When our momma sang us to sleep but now we're stressed out.

Another Rad Day

I wonder how much mileage I can get calling things "rad" over the next couple of months . . .

Lots happening for Greg at the cancer center on Thursday. He had an appointment at radiology for a CT scan and to make the mask that will be used for radiation. At his appointment on Monday, the doctor mentioned that his staples needed to come out before the CT and mask making, and that the radiology department could do the staple removal.

When Greg arrived on Thursday, there was a bit of confusion as there wasn't an appointment or order for staple removal. There was a Patient Navigator this time – she jumped to action and arranged for the staples to be removed. Before Greg left for staple removal, she handed him a 3-ring binder called, "Patient Guide to Duke Radiation Oncology." The chapters include things like Welcome, Phone Numbers, Getting Help, What to Expect, Social Work, Nutrition, and Pet Therapy. The "What to Expect" section is almost as fun as "What to Expect when You're Expecting" and includes things like fatigue, nausea and vomiting, swelling, sexual changes, and urinary and bladder changes (not all of these apply to brain radiation). When I note the similarities between the radiation binder and the pregnancy book, Greg poofs out his stomach and says, "Yes, even my belly is getting big and round."

After reviewing the notebook, we were ushered back to an exam room to a nurse. "My name is Anastasia" she says, holding up her badge. She was A+ – funny but not false; she was calm, confident, and very much at ease. She managed to hold up a surgical staple remover and say, "OK, I'm here to take out your bling" and not sound frightening or obnoxious. After three surgeries, the nerves along Greg's incision are fairly fried, so this staple removal was less bothersome than his first go-round. After pulling out a mere 60 staples, Anastasia placed a call to the CT room and Greg was off for mask making and scanning.

I learned that they create his mask and then run the CT with his mask in place. This lets the radiation oncologist create a map of his treatment dose using his exact anatomy. Greg's dad came for the appointments and stayed for the duration of Greg's time. Before Greg went in for the CT, I left for work. I told the CT technician that Greg would probably fall asleep. He's still having more awake time at night than he'd like, but the zzzs are moving in the right direction. I headed back to work knowing Greg was in good hands.

So, How Are the Kids?

People ask how Belle and Abe are doing. Even with the intense ups and downs of Greg's cancer diagnosis and treatment, we can almost always say, "The kids are great." They are active and vibrant. They ask great questions. They are honest. A week or so ago, Abe woke up at 2:45a to go to the bathroom. In the dark of the night, I hear him say, "I'm sad that Daddy has brain cancer." They ask why the first medicine didn't work. They ask if the new medicine will work better this time. They ask what happens if the cancer comes back again. They ask if cancer is contagious (we've covered this topic many, many times. They still ask). We answer as honestly as we can.

They follow our lead and talk about how great Duke's Brain Tumor Center is and how Dad, "has the best doctors in the world." Even with uncertainty, they accept and are calmed by our answers. Abe wears his tender-heartedness on his sleeve. He can be quick to cry. He worries about monsters and bad guys. He plays with toy weapons and attacks imaginary enemies. He's generally easy to calm and comfort (except for the time he went completely bonkers at the dentist – that was a bad one. The dentist says with a thin, flat lipped smile, "you can take him outside if you need to."). More often than not, he ends up in our bed at some time during the night. He is sweet and snuggly and peaceful. We don't mind. Belle is more stoic. She likes finding ways to be helpful (unless she's teasing her brother). She is working on a "super-secret" project at school with her teacher, related to Greg's cancer. We're excited to learn what it is.

It is tempting to chalk up their strong spirits to stellar parenting. However, I know that it has more to do with the circle of love and support that surrounds them. Greg and I are tattered at times, but our love is unconditional. Their teachers share a blessing for our family during morning prayer and don't deduct the 10% if homework is turned in a day late. My parents live nearby and help us with logistics (like lending a car) and keeping the kids for dinner when Greg and I need extra time. When Abe freaked out at the dentist, I brought him to their house to calm down. Noah ("Nuncle" to the kids), Yvonne ("Nant"), and baby Julia live in town and bring love and familiarity to Belle and Abe. The kids feel the love from family afar, with visits and phone calls, cards and birthday gifts. We've lived in the same house since the kids were born. Belle and Abe's lives are intertwined with our next-door friends and neighbors – they play together for hours and cry when they go more than 2 -3 days without seeing each other. They have welcomed Belle and Abe for sleepovers and we share many meals together. Our family, friends, neighborhood, school, work, and churches have built a fortress of love and support around us. If Belle or Abe start to fray, there is somebody to tend to the tear and weave the pieces together again.

Parenting is never an exercise in perfection. Belle and Abe's questions don't always have easy or comfortable answers. However, when my spirit drifts downward, Belle and Abe remind me of our strength. Their freckled cheeks that light up when they smile and the clumps of dirt left on the floor after they've stomped in frustration all remind me that I can't control the journey, but I can celebrate the warmth and gifts of our support.

Treatment Tomorrow

Greg starts chemo and radiation tomorrow. Debbie and Zachary flew in tonight and will be here for the week. They'll help with some of the juggling until Greg hopefully settles into a routine.

We picked up his 42 days of chemo from the cancer center pharmacy this morning. During one of the education sessions, they mentioned that he'd be on a low-dose of chemo every day for his 6-weeks. His chemo dose ended up being higher than we imagined – each daily dose is about

1/2 of what he took each day during the 5-day cycles he had in the past.

When he first learned that the tumor was growing again, we sat through an education session with the neuro-oncology nurse regarding the logistics and schedule. She reviewed the steps regarding when to take anti-nausea meds, when to stop eating, and when to take his chemo in relation to his radiation start time. I remember feeling a bit shell shocked during the teaching session. She gave us papers explaining everything. Since that session, Greg had his craniotomy and had several appointments with the radiation team. Each appointment involved lots of sheets of paper. Now, we can't find the papers the nurse gave us during the original teaching session. He can easily call to get the info again, but I have to chuckle a bit given that my job is a nurse care manager and I'm feeling overwhelmed by all of the papers poor Greg is getting.

Ask and Ye Shall Receive

"Until we can receive with an open heart, we're never really giving with an open heart. When we attach judgement to receiving help, we knowingly or unknowingly attach judgement to giving help."
~ Brené Brown

I often write about how grateful our family is for all the kind words and deeds showered on us as Greg has gone through multiple surgeries and treatment paths. My family has taught me the importance of accepting help from others with a gracious heart, hopefully without pretense or expectation. I often think of the golden rule, to do to others what you would want them to do to you. I ponder a twist to the rule – receive from others what you would want them to receive from you. My ability to give has been diminished since Greg's diagnosis. My ability to receive has expanded.

After his first two surgeries, we received many wonderful meals from friends, neighbors, coworkers, and family. I loved not having to plan dinner in the evening. As grateful I was for the food we received in the past, I didn't want to ask for food again after this surgery. Receiving is a verb, an action, and I was feeling vulnerable and depleted. When people asked what help we needed, my general response was, "we're doing OK now, thank you." Eventually, those near and dear to us wanted, needed, to offer a way to support us. A discussion led to the idea of receiving help for our firewood stash. Our wood burning stove goes through many, many stacks of wood each winter. Greg gathers wood in the spring and summer for the following winter – the real burners get two years ahead.

Word of our wishes got out and now our wood stacks are starting to fill. We have a huge pile of oak in the driveway and people have donated money for us to buy firewood. Our friend Drew and his family also heat with a woodburning stove. A couple of weekends ago, he arranged for a huge truckload of oak to be dropped off at our house. He then coordinated with our church to have people come help with splitting and stacking. When I saw the pile of rounds, taller than Belle, I thought there was no way the mound could be split and stacked in a day. Much to my amazement, four men got everything split and stacked by 11a. I was struck by the power of communal living. What would have taken weeks for Greg to manage alone was accomplished in a few hours by collective focus, strong muscles, and sharp mauls.

Greg has mixed feelings about the help train making a stop in firewood land. He takes pride in the physical labor and resulting warmth. He also enjoys the hunt for hardwood, the sweat of swinging the maul, and the meditative side of splitting and stacking. The work of firewood is much like the work of cooking and cleaning – whatever feels complete at the end of the day will need to be tackled again after the next sunrise. In the meantime, we are getting a jump on next winter's BTUs.

Greg's is one week into his chemo and radiation. The schedule of medications and getting to the cancer center is a lot to juggle every day, but he's managed so far. He is feeling more tired. Today, he was told to go ahead and get a special lotion to put on his skin at the radiation site.

Spring Break 2016 – Woo Hoo!!!

My devilish side is coming out this week. We have friends off on wild and wonderful spring break adventures. Facebook is filled with pictures of happy families at beaches and mountains, even jungles. I am tempted to do a Facebook post showing Greg at the cancer center getting a blood draw or preparing for treatment with a caption that reads, "Spring Break 2016, Woo Hoo!!" I won't. I am genuinely happy for my friends. Family Sousa has had many wonderful trips in the past and will have more wonderful trips in the future. No need for me to be snarky.

Greg is getting to his daily radiation appointments and tolerating chemo. He has started back to work. As I witness him navigate his day, I feel a mix of wonder and pride. After three surgeries and diving into a more challenging treatment path, Greg stays strong. He is biking, working, and participating in family activities.

Half-way Zapped

Greg is 1/2 way through his radiation. His appointments are in the morning. He's been able to go to work after treatment and do some bike commuting. He's even jumping into the BMX race season and has gotten in a couple of races. He's taking care of his skin, the area of treatment across his forehead taking on a slightly different hue. He says, 'I'm working on a focused suntan." He's tired and balancing a few GI issues, but of the list of possible problems, these seem relatively minor.

Belle competed in her State gymnastics meet this past Friday in Hickory, NC. She scored well in all events and qualified for Regionals in Tennessee. She is super excited, it's fun to see her grow physically and mentally through the season.

Bullet Points

- Not enough time to write.
- Sousas hanging in there.
- Greg had some bumps this past weekend.
- Puking sucks.
- Zofran is his friend.
- Belle fell and is in a sling for 10 - 14 days.
- Grami visiting.
- Grami has a great smile.
- Grami makes yummy soup.
- We got in another date night.
- Whisky Tango Foxtrot is a great movie.
- Greg is 2/3 through chemo/radiation.

Bumps

Part of growing up is learning to navigate life's struggles without losing your shit . . uh . . mind. Babies learn that heart-felt crying is a sure way to get some wanted or needed attention from an adult. Even now, Abe has a meltdown when he puts his shoes on and there is a bump in his sock. Belle used to be this way. Now, she is not. She's learned to take off her shoe, get her sock straightened out, and carry on. Eventually, we learn that in any given day, there is spilled coffee, grumpy friends or coworkers, computer glitches that strike moments before a presentation, and picnics cancelled because of thunderstorms. While frustrating for a moment, our mental health isn't jeopardized by these unwanted or unexpected shifts away from our best intentions.

Sometimes the bumps are bigger, throwing us off our game. Slicing a finger while making dinner, getting lost on the way to a job interview, dropping a phone in water, or breaking a cherished treasure. These bigger disruptions are still normal, still part of being human, but they sting. They sucker punch our sense of calm, send a ripple through joy. Still, within hours, or maybe days, we recover.

Being human comes with bigger heartbreaks and heartaches – divorce, hospitalizations, miscarriage, death of loved ones, natural disasters. Nobody goes to their grave without having lived through big hardships. Hopefully, these are infrequent – years ticking by between them. Unlike the little frustrations of daily living, we don't brush off or quickly bounce back from deep loss. It can take months or even years to process, understand, and recover from holes left in our hearts, our psyche. Sometimes, the physical and emotional toll changes how we think, how we interact with others, how we understand our place in the world.

Greg's cancer has been a big hit – a physical and emotional impact for us. When he was first diagnosed, I remember feeling like life would never return to the pre-cancer hum of our daily rhythms. A year later, I found solace in the places where our lives did indeed slide into the comforting rhythm of school, work, summer travel, making pancakes on the weekend, enjoying a cold beer on our stoop with neighbors. The impact of his cancer still had an imprint on our lives, but it wasn't front and center.

We're coming up on four years since his diagnosis. Across those years, he's had three craniotomies, one biopsy, months of chemotherapy, dozens of scans and blood work, medical appointments, and now weeks of more intensive radiation and chemotherapy. Much has changed since his cancer. The work of living with a major illness has changed how we think, how we act, how we see the world.

And, yet, much is still the same. Belle and Abe's freckles highlight their noses and cheeks in school pictures. Greg unclicks the lock on the bike shed, pulls out his favorite mode of transportation, and glides out the slight decline on our driveway headed to work. We enjoy weekends in the mountains or at the beach. The kids run and play outside, climbing trees and finding frogs and turtles. We almost always find time to come together at the end of the day and sit together for dinner. Two faith communities welcome us. Our trusty car carries our bikes and bodies where we need to go.

During these weeks of Greg's radiation and chemo, I struggle with the dichotomy of the hardship of what he is going through with the comforting daily rhythms and the places where joy is still very much present. I know how to be happy. I know how to be sad. I'm not doing very well with trying to be both at the same time. His doctors are want to gush about how wonderful he is doing with treatment, how he is able to work and bike, how well his skin is holding up, how his GI symptoms are relatively in check. I have a hard time shutting of the, "yes, but ... " voice in my head. Yes, but this is still a really hard time.

One of my least favorite times in church is the sharing of blessings and concerns. Somebody celebrated a wedding, somebody's aunt just got diagnosed with breast cancer, somebody wants to pray for Syrian refugees, somebody just became a grandmother, somebody's cousin's neighbor's dog died, and so on. The joys and hardships are ticked off around the congregation in a matter of minutes. My emotional clock starts to fritz and I feel grumpy. How the frick am I supposed to process others' experiences that are worthy of collective sharing, let alone bring God into the conversation? I find myself having a similar struggle with Greg's treatment. "Honey, I need to take my chemo before we take the kids to school." "Let me put my bike on the back of the car so that I can bike to work from radiation." "Let's see if we can get in a date night before my next MRI." Um, OK.

We still work hard to help Belle and Abe learn when it's OK to freak out and when it's better to roll with the bumps. You just fell and scraped a few layers of skin off your knees and palms – yes, go ahead and take some time. You lost your favorite shorts – don't worry, find a different pair, the old ones will turn up. We don't have waffles for breakfast – take a chill pill and eat some cereal instead. Your friend was mean to you today – let's sit and talk that through.

Three-plus years into Greg's brain tumor treatment, I reflect on what I need to learn. Holding the hardships and celebrating gifts at the same time is difficult and yet, has become a necessity for getting through the day. They don't magnify each other and they don't cancel each other out. They just sit there together. They share space and time – a complicated and confusing emotional ecosystem. More than anything, Greg needs the security of our joyful rhythms. More than anything, I need a safe place for my sadness and worry. More than anything, we need each other and the security of our family and wider circle to be with us through it all.

Finito

Greg completed chemo and radiation this past Thursday. I went to his Monday appointment for his doctor check-in and wasn't there on Thursday. He reports getting hugs and well wishes from his therapists (the folks running the machine) and his radiation oncologist came by to congratulate him and give him well wishes. Greg will transition back to his neuro oncology team and won't follow up with radiation oncology unless there is a particular concern or question.

We didn't do much of a celebration. Greg biked to work from treatment. The kids and I planned a nice dinner for him when he got home – a bouquet of flowers, dinner from his favorite restaurant, and an assortment of dark chocolate cupcakes with glistening white frosting.

Greg can get back into life's rhythm without having to fit in daily radiation. His GI system will hopefully settle and he'll get some energy back. The doctors said that it can take two weeks to get over the stronger effects of radiation.

His first post-treatment MRI is May 23rd. We're not sure what his doctors are planning – if he'll go back to the 2-month scans and check-ups or if there'll be additional chemo or some other therapy. We'll find out on the 23rd.

Would You Rather … .

Belle has taken to a word game that I'll call, "Would you rather?" She asks questions like these:

Belle: *Would you rather eat a worm or eat guinea pig poop?*
Me: *I'd rather eat guinea pig poop – I'd swallow that little turd like an Advil.*

Belle: *Would you rather be caught in a hurricane or a tornado?*
Me: *I'd rather be caught in a hurricane – been there, done that, lived to tell about it.*

Belle: *Would you rather win a million dollars or own a castle with 100 horses?*
Me: *I'd rather win a million dollars – duh, who wants a castle and a bunch of horses?*

It's a sweet and clever way to learn about the world around her and about adults she trusts.

A few days ago, out of the blue, she asks, "Would you rather have your arm bitten off by a shark or have a grade 3 brain tumor?" Well, then. We recently watched a movie called Soul Surfer. This movie depicts Bethany Hamilton, a girl who had her arm bitten off by a shark when she was 13. The movie is dramatic, poignant, and a bit bloody. Bethany struggles with the loss of her limb and goes on to brave the waters again to become a professional surfer. I imagine her life is difficult. She recently had a baby (she's now in her 20s). I wonder how she holds the baby and gets a glass of water at the same time.

Without hesitation, I answer my daughter: I'd rather have my arm bitten off by a shark.

I don't know much about shark attacks – just what I see in the news and movies. I know a bit about grade 3 brain tumors. Like the worm/guinea pig poop question, I really don't have all available data. However, in thinking about her question over the past few days, nothing makes me want to change my answer. In some ways, Bethany and Greg have a lot in common. They have survived a physical assault few people can ever understand. They are brave, they are strong, they are positive, they are filled with faith, they are survivors. Still, cancer casts a shadow like no other. Bethany's shark is long gone. Perhaps dead. Perhaps feasting on better things like grouper and tuna. Greg cancer still has a presence, still hovering about causing mischief and anxiety.

Maybe one day, I'll change my answer. Hopefully nobody I know will endure a shark attack. Hopefully, the boxing match with cancer will end with a victorious Greg. We'll tend to his wounds and recollect. Then, we can ponder what we'd do with a million dollars.

Post-radiation Appointment

Greg's scan today was stable – this is great news in the brain tumor world. He's got quite a cavity in his brain, now. Tomorrow, he will begin 6-months of daily, oral chemo. He will be on the same chemo he's been on before. He will be on a lower dose that he takes every day. The cumulative monthly dose will be greater than the monthly dose he was on during past chemo cycles. We're not too excited about that piece, but we understand. He will get blood work every two weeks, an oncology appointment every month, and an MRI every two months.

Scans

The first time I saw an image of the inside of Greg's brain, I was sitting on the curb outside of a CVS in suburban Atlanta. I was with a close friend who happened to be an emergency department doctor. Greg was inside picking up seizure medicine. We met in Atlanta after his seizure and ED visit in Alabama. He carried a computer disc with the results of a CT scan done in Alabama. He was to bring the disc to his doctor in Durham, to determine next steps. The AL doctors said that the scan showed a lesion.

I remember having no idea what the term "lesion" meant. My friend had her laptop with her. She said, "We can look at the images, if you want." She placed the disc in her machine. Cars drove through the shimmering, hot parking lot while her computer whirred with the sound of loading information.

When the images came up, we were speechless for a moment. After a few seconds, I might have said something along the lines of, "fuck, what is that?" My friend said that she didn't know. In hindsight, she must have known, being an ED doctor in a major metropolitan city. But she was being a good friend. She wasn't there to diagnose, but to provide emotional support. She might have been willing to diagnose some things, but not a brain tumor in her dear friend's husband. She wasn't lying – there was no way she could know what type of brain tumor Greg had. The wisp of a lesion I'd imagined was in fact an egg-sized mass of different shades and shapes, taking over the right, front side of his brain. Greg got his medication and we headed back to Durham.

Since that day, Greg and I have seen dozens of images of his brain. He's had an MRI every two months for the past four years, even more around his surgeries. He graduated to a three month scan only one time.

Then, a small spot put him on watch and he went to one and then back to two month time increments.

Reviewing the MRIs is still unsettling. His initial surgery left him with an empty space tucked behind his right eye where brain and then tumor once were. After a biopsy and two more surgeries, his right lateral ventricle now opens into a gaping hole.

Greg is active and engaged in the brain tumor community. We know many survivors, some of whom share their MRI images, posting pictures on Facebook or blogs after good or sometimes bad news. If I'd seen Greg's MRI ten years ago, I might have thought that the damage was incompatible with life. At the very least, I would have thought that the owner of such disrupted cerebral tissue would suffer some terrible disability. Now, I know that brain tumor patients are surprisingly alive, active, and engaging. At Greg's most recent oncology appointment, we were in the waiting room with another survivor and friend (same doctor, same appointment date and time. Go figure). Later, his wife posted pictures of their visit. This friend has the same tumor type as Greg, but his is inoperable. He's gone through chemo and radiation. The MRI is astounding. It shows a huge mass taking over what appears to be almost the whole left side of this brain. The tumor is like an octopus – tentacles twisting in, through, and around his brain's sulci. I can't wrap my own brain around the image. It truly doesn't seem possible. You could be behind this person at the grocery store and never know there was a problem. He bears no scars. He walks, talks, and makes jokes with ease. Everything in his appearance and movement is symmetrical. He is funny. He talks about events in the past. He articulates thoughts about the future. Like Greg, his feet, his heart, his spirit are firmly planted in the here and now.

For the moment, the images of Greg's brain will keep coming. We'll keep processing the information. Stable is good – no new growth. Spots can be bad – mischievous cells sucking up contrast and giving up their hiding place to diligent oncologists. Either way, the magic and mystery of neurons continue to connect and pulse, making Greg our biking, laughing, loving Greg.

Intermediate

Belle had her regional gymnastics meet in Tennessee. Belle, my mom, and I drove to Tennessee. Greg and Abe drove separately, stopping for Greg to race in a BMX race in Charlotte, then meeting us for Belle's meet.

There are four main divisions in BMX racing: novice, intermediate, expert, and professional. A rider must win 10 races in his/her class to advance to the next class. Greg had won nine races at the novice level. Winning in Charlotte would give him his tenth win to move to intermediate.

Before driving to Tennessee, Greg called with good news. He won his race, meeting the criteria to move up to intermediate class. He is a badass.

Innumerable, June 2016

Dookity Dan

I'll explain the story of the "Dookity Dan" title later, it provides some comic relief to our last 24 hours.

The short version (of the past week, not of Dan) is that Greg strained his back while chopping wood on May 21st. He went to urgent care on Monday June 6th and received antibiotics for a possible urinary tract infection. He went to primary care on Wednesday June 8th because he was still having the same symptoms that brought him to urgent care. The primary care doctor noted that his bladder was extremely full and sent him to the ED. I didn't realize urinary retention was considered a medical emergency until they whisked him back into a room and used an ultrasound machine to measure the amount of urine in his bladder. When the machine showed the highest possible reading, they inserted a catheter and ordered an MRI, stat. The MRI showed lesions on his spine.

So . . .

We've moved from the smaller community ED to Duke Hospital's big ED. We've been sitting in the ED waiting for a bed to open on the neuro floor to figure out what is going on and what is next. We've met with the on-call neuro-oncologist and await a visit from Greg's primary neuro-oncologist.

Mr. Sousa

Greg has been at the cancer center for four years. He's a friendly guy, so within short time, much of the Brain Tumor Center staff would holler "Hey Greg" with a smile as he navigated his appointments. Once or twice, when the news wasn't as rosy, he became Mr. Sousa. The first time, we were taken off guard. His normally warm and smiling "Hey Greg" oncologist was suddenly calling him "Mr. Sousa" – it was totally weird.

Unfortunately, it's been a "Mr. Sousa" couple of days. He was supposed to get an MRI last night. With contrast dye, a person can't have more than one MRI within 24 hours. He had an MRI with contrast at the first ED, so the staff at Duke had to wait 24 hours for the 2nd MRI. The order was put in as "regular" instead of "stat" and he kept getting bumped to the bottom of the schedule. This morning, his radiologist changed the order to stat and he got the brain and spine imaging done. Soon after getting back to his room, the doctor came in to do a spinal tap – the same doctor who screwed the cage into his head for his biopsy. His team is collecting spinal fluid for pathology.

The MRI shows lesions along his whole spine – the oncologist called them "drop mets" – cancer cells dropping from the brain down into the spinal column. This is bad. They won't develop a treatment plan until pathology comes back, as they need to be confident about what they're treating. They want to rule out something unexpected like metastasized testicular cancer. He's on steroids to control swelling. The Brain Tumor Center is all-hands-on-deck right now with Greg – we are comforted by the intensity, the focus, the attention he is receiving from his medical team.

We sit tight. Greg might get to go home in the next couple of days. The kids leave tomorrow for a week at the beach with my NC parents.

Greg is finally in a deep sleep. He received some pain and anti-anxiety medicine prior to the lumbar puncture. I'm happy to see him resting.

Quiet Day

After yesterday's scans and spinal tap, today was relatively quiet. I slept at home with the kids last night – all together in Greg's and my big bed. I spent the morning packing the kids up for the beach – bundles of goggles and towels and sunscreen serving to distract me from the bubble of anxiety agitating my core. They headed off with my parents around lunch and I went to the hospital to visit Greg. I missed the morning rounds with the doctors, but there wasn't much new to report.

They're still trying to get Greg's bladder working again. He is on steroids to reduce swelling in his spine. They hope that this will get the nerves into his bladder working again. They've also been playing around with his fluids and sodium a bit. He's staying at the hospital tonight. He was happy to receive visitors. He's been walking laps around the floor. His appetite is down a bit, but he's enjoying fresh fruit.

I'll sleep at home tonight and then head back to the hospital in the morning.

Home

We are back home and Greg gets to sleep in his own bed tonight.

Back at Big Duke

Our time at home was short lived. Greg had a bumpy evening. He managed to make it up the stairs last night for bed, but found that his legs weren't working to get him back down the stairs in the morning. He ended up having to scoot down on his bottom, like a toddler. I called the doctor around 5a and she advised us to go back to the ED. We met with the doctor there and now Greg is back in the hospital.

Greg's pathology came back showing that his primary brain tumor metastasized into his spine. The doctors are going to do some radiation to his spine and give him two new chemotherapy drugs. He'll be at the hospital to see if the radiation gets some of his symptoms under control.

Goals

Goals are important. They give us drive and motivation to move forward, to make the future better than the past. When I work with patients, I spend time helping them develop a goal. I've had many trainings on how to create SMART goals – Specific, Measurable, Achievable, Realistic, Time-bound. Not, "My diabetes will get better." but "I will check by blood sugar three times a day for five of the next seven days and keep a log of the results to discuss with my nurse."

We have two goals right now.

1. Greg will be discharged from the hospital tomorrow.
2. Greg and I will be able to have our date night at The Durham Hotel on Friday evening.

Greg's doctors are aware of these goals and are working to help us meet them.

Greg's mom and sister are here. They drove down from RI. They are setting up camp at an Extended Stay hotel and will be with us as Greg's treatment path unfolds. Greg's sister has work obligations and his mom still has two treatments for her cancer back in RI, but we'll hopefully have some extra family by our side in the weeks ahead.

As always, Greg manages to bring laughter into the space around him. I'll share the explanation of the Dookity Dan story. Last Wednesday, the first doctor who saw us at the Duke Hospital ED introduced himself as Dan. He said hello to us and then promptly got paged. He stepped into the hallway to answer the page, saying, "Duke E.D., Dan." Greg says, "Wait, didn't he say his name is Dan? It sounded like he just said his name was Dookity." We quickly realized that Duke ED became Dookity and had to chuckle. The rest of the night, the nursing staff would come in and reminisce on our doctor, "Dookity Dan" and laugh. The doctor's new nickname made the rounds at the ED and gave lots of people a chuckle.

Greg had a disheartening physical therapy consult. The nerves feeding his legs have taken a hit from the tumors. For now, his life will be limited to the downstairs portion of our house. We have a bed downstairs, but no shower or bathtub. We'll be looking to have a ramp built or installed that will get him in our front door. We're bummed at this turn. The hope is that the chemo and radiation will quiet down the tumors and bring some life back to the nerves in his lower spine.

Check!

We can check our first goal off the list, Greg is safely home.

The last two days at the hospital were hectic with appointments and planning meetings (along with meds, catheterizations, neuro checks, and other fun things). We have most everything in line except for a ramp for our front steps, which is in progress (we hope).

Without a ramp, we were stuck figuring out how to get Greg up our three front steps into the house. As we were driving home, we called several neighbors to ask for assistance getting in the house, but were unsuccessful in finding anybody who was home. When we pulled up to our house, we saw Greg's mom, our next-door neighbor, and her sister. Our next-door neighbor had a baby on June 6th and her sister is visiting from Phoenix. Greg initially called all male neighbors, to tap into their physical strength in lifting him. When he saw the three women, he made a funny comment about all the men he'd called. Something along the lines of, "Look, there are my men."

The lucky stars were shining brightly upon Casa Sousa. We learned that our neighbor's sister works as a physical therapist in neurology. She knew exactly how to get Greg into the house using the resources we had – she patiently explained how to move each leg, how to use the rail for support, and how to balance and adjust his weight to move his body up the steps. Later, when Greg had trouble getting up out of a reclining chair, she came over and gave some great tips on getting up out of chairs.

Great Date

We are back from our awesome date night. I'll write more on that later, but in sum, it was perfect.

Happy Father's Day

The Durham Date: As part of our date night, we had dinner and drinks on The Durham Hotel's rooftop restaurant. It was unusually cloudy, windy, and cool. Greg was happy to not be in the humid heat that is normal for June in NC. We had a mix of small plates and enjoyed a cocktail and beer. We went to bed early. Our original room was not handicapped accessible. When I asked the front desk if they had a plastic chair or stool for the shower, they offered to move us into a room with a wheelchair accessible bathroom. We happily agreed.

Our room was quiet and calm, just what we needed. Greg had a bouquet of flowers delivered for me – it was the size of my head, layers of yellow, red, and purple. The bed was just the right firmness with lots of fluffy pillows. We crashed early. Greg is tossy, turny at night, but is doing better than he did at the hospital.

After an OK night's sleep, we went down for breakfast. The Durham serves food prepared with local ingredients – we had fruit, granola, oatmeal, crazy good bacon, and a strawberry corn muffin.

After our lovely stay, we moseyed home to meet the kids.

Greg: Greg is holding steady. The doctor described his experience last week as "a free fall." His medical team has stopped the free fall and Greg is getting by at home. He'll get up and about for a bit and then lay down to rest. His legs are sore and tired, mostly on the left. We're hoping that his spine and legs will release to improve his walking and urinary symptoms.

Party Time: Before the craziness of the past couple of weeks, I wanted to throw a birthday party for Greg. I planned to call it something along the lines of, "Throw Last Year in the Trash Bash." He had two craniotomies and one biopsy over the past year, plus chemo and radiation, big ugh. Greg's birthday is June 7th and mine is June 28th, so a June party seemed in order.

I rented the pavilion at a city park. The original plan was to coordinate friends and family to gather for food and use of the playground and pump track. We're still going to have a party, but there will be much less planning.

Hard Work

Being sick is hard work. Day-to-day activities like getting dressed, brushing teeth, going to the bathroom, and eating require a new level of focus, effort, and energy. These tasks that are normally mindless and fluid are carefully broken into incremental steps requiring planning and often assistance. We are busy managing medications (which are still changing), getting to appointments, scheduling and receiving home visits from physical therapy, and monitoring symptoms. We have new equipment at home like a walker and catheters. I am trying to work a regular schedule and Greg is figuring out how to best stay connected with work while managing his time away. We are tired.

Greg's mobility is slowing getting better. His gait is smoother. He can sit up for longer stretches. He enjoys getting out here and there for a meal or an errand. Seeing him reclaim pieces of his function lifts our spirits. He had bloodwork and a check-in with the mid-level oncologist on Monday. She is happy with where he is at and will continue to keep a close eye on him, with regular bloodwork and visits. His next MRI is August 8th.

The highlight of our week was the birthday gathering. Friends, family, neighbors, and coworkers gathered under the pavilion at our nearby city park – cool cement flooring, green municipal picnic tables, and a simple, vaulted roof with wood beams. The picnic area is surrounded by a big playground, a bicycle pump track, basketball courts, and plenty of green space. People brought food and drinks. We saw friends we hadn't seen for a while, as well as tried and true faces who have been steadfastly by our side. Hugs and earnest offerings of help refilled our empty tanks.

We're gearing up for a big week. Thursday, Belle and I drive to Hershey, PA to meet close friends from Canada whom we haven't seen in a while. Hershey, PA happens to be mid-way between Durham, NC and Ottawa, Ontario. The trip is a gift for Belle from Greg for her 10th birthday. She and I will then drive to RI on Sunday for a week. Greg and Abe fly to RI on Saturday to meet us. Greg's friend, Fred, flew down from RI to visit and will fly back with Greg and Abe. My Mom is also going to fly up to RI with them. My boys will be in good hands.

Fred arrived today and is already a calming presence in the house. He and Greg have had a close friendship for decades, sharing deep moments of bumps and bruises, love and laughter. He is calm, earnest, helpful, and caring – he is not only happy, but honored to help our family – to bring Greg water, to sit and share stories of crazy BMX rides from decades ago. Fred is also a firefighter and can easily manage Greg's physical needs and any emergencies that may arise.

Travel Updates

At the moment, Greg is resting on his parents' couch and the kids are off to Legoland Boston with family. Belle's and my Hershey trip was perfect – the weather, the setting, the park, the activities, the chocolate, and most of all, the company. We wouldn't change a single thing. Even after a few years apart, Belle and her friend clicked immediately and had fun buying matching outfits and tearing through the amusement park. Hershey Park was crowded, but we never had to wait more than about 20 minutes for a ride and often we could just walk right on. There is a wide array of activities – roller coasters, a water park, gardens, games, and more. The girls hooked onto a ride called The Comet, but did lots and lots of other roller coasters and activities.

We met up with Greg and Abe at Greg's parents in RI on Sunday. Greg's friend Fred and his family were instrumental in making Greg's trip to RI smooth. Greg's parents set up a bedroom for us downstairs. We spent most of our time visiting friends and family. I took the kids to a bit of the parade on the 4th of July. We then went to a couple of gatherings of friends and family. Greg has a massive network here and he's working hard to connect with people he loves.

Greg is spending most of his time resting and visiting. He's focusing on all of his "cans" as opposed to his "can'ts." Even with physical limitations, he's getting out, eating well, and enjoying time to share stories and memories.

The Play Button

During Greg's last hospitalization, one of his neuro-oncologists described him as being in a clinical free fall. New symptoms developed quickly such as leg weakness and difficulty urinating. A week in the hospital and an array of new drugs hit pause on his decline. None of Greg's symptoms disappeared, but they stayed steady or improved slightly. No new symptoms presented themselves. Greg's doctors delivered tough news. They could work to keep his symptoms at bay, but they could no longer treat his cancer. The new drugs were intended to reduce swelling and slow the cancer's growth. Unfortunately, they wouldn't make the cancer go away.

With Greg holding steady, we decided to go ahead with the Hershey and Rhode Island trip. In light of his cancer's more fierce presence, Greg felt strongly about taking the time to connect with the people who have filled his soul since childhood, some since birth. He covertly called the trip his "palliative tour." We coordinated logistics to accommodate Belle's and my trip to Hershey. Greg's friend Fred flew down to be a guiding and steady presence for Greg and Abe's travels north. My Mom also flew up with them, to add her love and another set of helping hands. I felt confident about his well-being.

A few days into our trip, Greg's beastly, metastasized anaplastic oligodendroglioma decided to hit the play button again on his free fall. His bowel and bladder problems grew worse, his legs grew weaker, he started complaining of headaches, and he needed to lay down with eyes closed for most of the day. His appetite dropped and he became bothered by light and sound. Perhaps most concerning, after years of being an impressively lucid brain tumor patient, he started becoming confused and disoriented. Abe said, "I don't like it when daddy is confused, that's even worse than your pee being broken." Greg spent most of his days being still and quiet, getting up for brief moments to eat and visit with loved ones.

I contacted Greg's doctors to give them an update. We decided we needed to get back to Durham sooner. I was worried that if we went to an ED in RI, he would be admitted and we'd be stuck in unfamiliar territory without the comfort of his regular medical team. I contacted the airline and switched our tickets to return home a day early. His doctors said that they'd alert the weekend neuro-oncology team at Duke that we'd be coming in. Belle and Abe would return with Greg's sister on the original flight.

Getting ready for Greg's flight home was stressful. He fell more than once and had an episode of vomiting. I worried that we wouldn't make it. After lying still during the day, he tossed and turned most of the night restless and anxious. I desperately wanted us to be back in the comfort and safety of home. My stomach and heart were in knots of uncertainty. I initially thought that I could manage the flight back with Greg alone. Then, I realized I was in over my head and we booked a next-day ticket for Greg's dad to fly down with us.

After an anxious but relatively uneventful night, Greg, his dad, and I boarded a plane to head home. We juggled a wheelchair and change of planes in BWI. Poor Greg couldn't get comfortable during the layover and ended up laying on the ground of the boarding area to rest. He was shivering and I bought him a cheap travel blanket and expensive Baltimore sweatshirt.

We triumphantly made it back to Durham, going straight from the airport to the ED. He just came back from a CAT scan, the nurse is drawing blood, and we're waiting to talk to the neuro-oncologist.

For all the stress and worry of the trip, I'm happy that we ventured to RI. Greg put his heart and soul into connecting with his deep, powerful fabric of love. He saw cousins, aunts, uncles, family friends, parents of family friends, BMX friends, neighbors, and friends from his undergraduate years. He couldn't converse much and spent a lot of time lying down, but he was bathed in love and warmth and smiles and hugs. His childhood friends Fred and his wife were by our side for much of the trip, offering solid support and a blanket of comfort over our worry. Everybody put their needs aside to focus on our well-being.

Now, we wait for the next part of our exhausting, achy journey. This cancer has kicked some serious ass, but it hasn't taken our fighting hero down yet. Greg is still able to crack, some jokes here and there, bringing smiles to hospital staff. When a nurse asked him if he knew who I was, he replied, "Big Mama." She laughed and said, "OK, I'll take that."

Under Pressure

After landing at the airport, we spent all night and much of the day in Duke's ED. During the night, Greg had two seizures and remained quite agitated. He pulled out his IVs, continually yanked on his cardiac leads, and even kept trying to pull out his catheter (ouch).

Greg's CT scan showed a buildup of fluid in his brain. The ventricles in his brain were about 50% bigger than his last MRI. This is a big change and explains his new symptoms – the headaches, confusion, and other concerns. The doctors think that the tumors in his spine are blocking the flow of his cerebral spinal fluid. There is a procedure they can do to relieve the pressure, but it is an invasive procedure that requires another brain surgery and an ICU stay. The surgery would do nothing to prevent the underlying problem or to change the progress of his cancer.

After talking with his doctors and with family, we decided to move Greg into hospice care. We believe the best direction is to help him be as comfortable as possible. He has suffered so much over the past year. He deserves relief from the torment of his cancer.

Belle and Abe fly home this evening with Greg's sister. I leave shortly to meet them at the airport. Greg's dad will stay with him at the hospital and I'll be home with the kids. Right now, Greg is back at the Duke Medical Pavilion. We've completed intake with Transitions LifeCare for inpatient hospice. He will initially go to their inpatient facility. If his pain and agitation can be controlled, then he may go home and receive hospice care at home.

Off to fetch our wee ones. I'm ready to give them hugs and kisses and talk to them about Daddy.

Settled

We're mostly holding it together. Today, we had a special time with Father Chris from Immaculate Conception Church. He came to be with Greg for the Anointing of the Sick. Greg was supposed to arrive to the facility around 1pm, so Fr. Chris came around 1:15p. Unfortunately, Greg's ambulance was delayed until almost 3p. Fr. Chris was generous with his time and visited with me and Greg's dad and sister until Greg arrived. Greg then received the sacrament. We shared tears of sadness and relief. Greg did the sign of the cross a couple of times during the sacrament – after lying still for hours, his hand floated into the air, marking the shape of the cross. His actions were beautiful and powerful – the strength of his faith poured out of him, even through the cloud of his cancer and brain swelling. Greg's dad left for the airport after Fr. Chris left.

Later in the day, the kids and I came to visit Greg with my parents. Greg was sound asleep most of the visit. It was nice to see him and sad to leave. His sister will sleep in his room at hospice this evening.

It's too late for me to write much about how we are doing. The grief is deep. We have so many people walking with us right now. I'm trying to balance my grief, the children, financial logistics, work schedules, FMLA, visitors, medical paperwork, and more.

Unknown to us until recently, dear friends set up a bank account for us to help with medical bills and other unexpected expenses. It's super awkward to ask for money, but we know that people want to help and we have thousands of dollars of medical and other bills. Greg is surrounded by deep, shimmering, comforting love.

Mr. Popular

Poor Greg needed to lie down so badly during our layover in BWI. There were no couches in the terminal, so he made do on the ground. Along these lines, we've decided that we need to put some parameters around his visits at hospice. We very much want people to visit and know that Greg would want the same. We are asking that friends limit visit time to about 10 minutes and to no more than 3 people at a time. There is a beautiful sunroom and gardens at the facility that can help with the flow, if needed.

The kids and I slept in Greg's room at the hospice home last night. Belle and Abe are holding up extremely well. Abe still wears his heart on his sleeve while Belle is more mysterious. They each seemed to enjoy the evening with their dad. I plan to visit each day and will hopefully spend the night on Friday.

Greg had a good day. The room was flooded with the warmth and love of visitors. After I left, he received a Reiki session which I heard brought a palpable, calming energy to Greg and to the room. I also missed some friends who sang to him. I am happy knowing that when I am away, he still has company and gifts of touch and voice. I am troubled by a very mysterious wound that appeared on his left thumb. The bottom of his nail bed is deep purple and swollen and his whole thumb is swollen and red. The wound appeared today and nobody can figure out what happened. He's had somebody with him 24/7, so it is really odd. The doctor took a look and agreed it was peculiar. The staff will keep an eye on it. On a good note, he took some sips of water. He clearly wanted the sips and was clear when he'd had his fill.

Everybody has been kind to ask how I am doing. I don't have a good answer. Most of the time, I'm on autopilot. My grief is more of a constant whisper than a loud roar. I've shed tears, but find myself surprisingly calm. I am less sad seeing Greg resting in bed, clearly deteriorating, than I am remembering his times of laughter and vitality. Yesterday I saw a picture of him laughing with Belle when she was a baby and my heart just broke. In thinking about my relative calm, I realize that I am physically and mentally exhausted from the past year. I am also buoyed by his strong presence. I can't deny where he is at right now. Even so, when I'm with him, I feel so connected to his spirit. I love his warm skin and dented forehead. I love when he moves his hand when somebody is talking, eyes closed. I love seeing his eyes when they flutter open for a brief moment. Today, giving him sips of water was so fulfilling in so many ways. I anticipate the roar of grief will come. In the meantime, I appreciate people checking in and offering prayers and hugs.

Last Breath – July 14, 2016

The saddest face I've ever seen was when Greg's doctors came into his hospital room to share that they no longer had any treatment options to fight his cancer. He was resting in the bed after a grueling week of tests and scans. The news completely, utterly broke him. His face, so clearly connected to his heart, collapsed. Imagine a full, vibrant balloon connected to the end of a vacuum. All joy was immediately sucked away. Greg was physically, emotionally, and mentally prepared to fight this disease as long as he possibly could. When the best doctors in the world blazing in the dazzle of "We Got Hope" suddenly shift to an empty, sad "we got nothing", everything changes. Everything.

His cancer, not the most aggressive type, was not supposed to spread, to metastasize. Doctors don't even scan the spines of patients with his tumor type because there is such little concern for metastasis. The first MRI of his whole spine showed tumors from his cervical spine all the way down into his lumbar spine. The nerves that spill out from the base of the spine into the legs are called the cauda equina, like a horse's tail. Normally, the thin filaments cannot be well seen on imaging. His lit up brightly, coated in tumor cells. The radiologist wrote that the tumors were innumerable. Not eight, not a few, not several, not even many, but innumerable. Everybody was floored. We learned that his primary oncologist had to take a few moments to collect herself after seeing the images. The scans also showed new, inoperable tumors in his brain. I have a hard time imagining how he was able to function with a spine full of tumors. Only our Greg.

After being discharged home, Greg held onto every last morsel of hope. He mentioned his new deficits as quickly and efficiently as possible and then focused on what he could do and what he wanted moving forward. After battling urinary retention for weeks, he celebrated when a few drops of urine came out on their own. After losing the ability to walk up stairs, he smiled broadly when he started to be able to lift his leg a few inches off the ground. He dove into planning our trip to Rhode Island. He was somehow able to honor the gravity of his disease's progression while still carrying the light of his planning and dreaming for the future.

Greg hoped to have a moment of reprieve, even improvement, before the disease continued to chip away at his function. He wanted to return to work, he wanted to volunteer at the BMX track, he wanted to make videos for Belle and Abe that they could play at their weddings one day, he wanted to get our finances organized, he wanted to ride his BMX bike again, "Even if I just have to coast out of the gate." None of these came to pass.

Greg's days in hospice went so very fast. I really, really didn't want him to go so quickly on this last part of his journey. He was admitted to hospice on Sunday July 10th and died the morning of the 14th. His days at Transitions LifeCare were flooded with visitors pouring their love and energy into him. Once the flow of visitors was tamed to a calm progression, his spirit relaxed and he seemed to enjoy the presence of others. We were able to bear witness to how much love and kindness he generated. The goal of hospice care is to get the patient home for their final days. Greg was never stable enough to be discharged home. I have mixed feelings about this, but realize that it would have been tremendously difficult for me to manage his symptoms, the kiddos, and the number of people visiting him. Transitions managed his care the way a conductor manages an orchestra, each component of his care aligned and in sync to maximize his gifts and his comfort.

The kids and I spent the night with Greg on Monday the 11th. The evening was surprisingly similar to our evenings at home when we sometimes all slept in the same room for a Sousa slumber party. The kids wrestled and bickered a bit, I had to ask them to brush their teeth 10 times, they arranged their stuffed animals just so, I sang bedtime songs, and we settled into the night. Belle and Abe were not overtly distressed at Greg's condition and took pleasure in his errant snores and when he moved his hands and arms in response to something. Abe slept right through the night-time visits from nurses to turn Greg and catheterize him. Belle and I woke with each visit but seemed to return to sleep. The kids were disappointed that they couldn't spend another night with him at hospice.

I planned to sleep with Greg at hospice on Friday night, this time without the kids. I wanted an evening with him, without the distractions of our little ones. Each day during the week, we could see him slowing down. On Wednesday, I stepped out of his room and asked his nurse if my plans to sleep over on Friday might be too late. Hospice has learned to never put a timeline on a patient's journey. She did say that she thought I'd be OK to sleep over on Friday.

Around 8pm on Wednesday evening, his nurse called me to report that his temperature had climbed to 104 and his was breathing around 40 breaths for minute (normal is 12 – 20). She said that she gave him Tylenol, placed ice around him, and repositioned him. She would call me in an hour. We talked again around 9:30p and she said that his temp was down to 101 but he was still breathing fast. I decided to come in. Auntie Debbie and her friend Jess stayed with the kids and I headed to hospice. My NC dad, lending his calming presence to Greg, left after I got there.

The nurses positioned him to the side of the bed and allowed me to lie next to him for the night. He was mostly bare but because the room was so cold, I snuggled next to him under a pile of blankets. We stayed together the whole evening. His breathing remained fast, but he was otherwise calm and relaxed. The nurses came in periodically to check on us and give his medications. With the lights turned off, I sang each of Belle and Abe's bedtime songs to him. My breath didn't cry, but tears flowed. We then settled into the quiet of the night. Several times during the evening, I was overcome with an intense, physical sense of peace. The tension that had built over the past few weeks completely melted away, vanishing for a moment.

Around 4a, the nurse came in and elevated the head of the bed to see if that would help slow his rapid breathing. Almost immediately, his breathing slowed to almost normal. He remained relaxed after that. I leaned my head against his, so that his neck wouldn't crick too far to the left. Over the next hour or two, his breathing slowed and at 6:13a, it stopped.

I've heard that the last few moments before death can be hard for others present. I've heard about "death rattles" and "agonal breathing." I fully expected to experience a time when Greg would struggle to breathe at the end. The biggest rattles I heard were ones suggesting that perhaps he should clear his throat. During the last couple of hours, the nurses came in and offered his Ativan and morphine. I asked them to hold the meds, as he already seemed so at-ease. He was calmed by sitting up, not by medications. There were no agonal breaths, no strained movements or gestures or expressions. His last breath was completely relaxed. I know that he did not want to leave. His heart and his passions were immeasurably bigger than his tumors. Still, as the sun rose and his breaths slowed, he didn't fight. Our last evening together was the biggest gift he ever could have given and I am forever grateful.

Eulogy

In Sara's Words

In getting ready for today, I was asked to estimate the number of people who might be here. I had no idea. My Dad and I made a list of Greg's different circles. There are many. Our Fortunes Ridge neighborhood, his work at the City of Durham, my work at Duke, Durham Area Masters Aquatics, Carolina Godiva Track Club, Toastmasters, University of Rhode Island, University of Florida, TriGators, Immaculata Catholic School, Capital City BMX, Eastern Ramp Association, Touisset Rd., Coomer Ave., Pilgrim United Church of Christ, Bull City Running, and the Tisch Brain Tumor Center. I'm sure there are more.

Over the days and weeks to come, people from these circles will share stories of their time with Greg. Today, I can speak best about him and me. I can speak to the emptiness left behind and to how to help fill that space.

Greg and I were not a case of opposites attract. We also weren't two peas in a pod. We met through mutual friends and flowed into a deep friendship and relationship. Saying yes after he proposed was effortless, I could not imagine life without him. I still can't.

My first memory of him is when I was on crutches and he helped carry my laundry to the car. For Greg, helping others was like breathing. One of my most recent memories was when we were driving, late to school. There was a stalled car, blocking traffic. Greg said, "we should stop and help push." My first reaction was, "no." We were running late, someone else would eventually stop. Greg stopped and jumped out. He talked with the owner and they started pushing the car to the side. The driver was flustered and had the emergency brake on. Greg released the brake. The driver of a semi-truck behind us also came out and they pushed the car out of traffic. We might have been a couple of minutes late to school, but the kids and I were reminded of how easy it is to help others. Two or three minutes of our time made a big difference in one person's day.

For all that he offered, it was hard for Greg to receive. I'm pretty sure he'd be horrified by the financial help we've received in the past week. I'm also sure that he would be first in line to help a friend's family in the same situation. In his last few weeks, out of necessity, he allowed others to tend to some of his most basic needs. His engineering brain was sometimes overly precise in his requests, "Can you get me the pink cup on the left with 1/3 apple juice 2/3 water, please." He was constantly saying, "I'm sorry." This constantly broke my heart.

Last week, Belle and Abe lost their father. My greatest wish is that we remind them who this amazing Greg Sousa was. I can start cutting our grass, balancing our checkbook, and taking them to races and ramp parks. Perhaps one day I'll learn to swing a maul. There is still so, so much from Greg that I cannot do. Greg never forgot a name. He could meet you once in line to pick up a race number and remember your name forever more. I'm terrible with names, to the point of embarrassment. When you see us out and about now, remind us your name. Between the three of us, we might get by.

Greg loved making people laugh and he was good at it. I'm the serious one. At the end of the day, he'd get me to let out a big guffaw and then say, "I made you laugh! I love it when I make you laugh." I remember his tried and true jokes. I can't remember the jokes he spun in an instant, leaving a wake of smiles. If it weren't for Greg, I'd sit around with a box of tissues watching *Brokeback Mountain* instead of relaxing and laughing with *Pootie Tang* or *Strange Brew*. Belle, Abe, and I need you to help us laugh at life's quirky moments, during those unexpected times when pieces of our lives misalign and throw us off.

Greg was patient. In our family, he'd definitely get the, "Least likely to get flustered" award. I let my temper flare. Ask the kids about our broken cabinet, right at foot level. I can't stand the thought of our house without his steady, calm influence. As we go about our days, Belle, Abe, and I need you to remind us what it looks like to take a breath, to not engage with frustration. We need this not during a church meditation, but when we've lost something needed for the next step or when a trusted item breaks.

One of Greg's smallest circles was one he never wanted to be a part of. A brain tumor survivor. Being part of this circle revealed his most powerful gift. The motto of the Tisch Brain Tumor Center is, "At Duke, There is Hope." I was never at ease with this emphasis on hope. Greg's disease was brutal, he never got a break. The one time he progressed from two month to three month scans, his MRI showed a tiny spot. His doctors watched the spot closely, and eventually had his second of three craniotomies. Over the past four years, I was often pulled towards a quote from Ann Patchett's book State of Wonder, "Hope is a horrible thing, you know. I don't know who decided to package hope as a virtue because it's not. It's a plague. Hope is like walking around with a fishhook in your mouth and somebody just keeps pulling it and pulling it."

Somehow, through everything, Greg never, ever gave up hope. During our last week in Rhode Island, I called his doctor. When Greg heard me say to her, "He's showing some new deficits," he said with disbelief, "New deficits? What do you mean new deficits?" He still had every intention of improving. Lying in bed, eyes heavy with fatigue below his dented forehead, he had plans to return to work, walk up stairs, and ride his bike. He wanted to make videos for Belle and Abe that they might play at their wedding. He wanted to write letters for them to read before getting their driver's license. He had big plans.

Since Greg died, I've realized that an aching, scary, angry hope is infinitely better than no hope at all, than the emptiness of being hopeless. With family, friends, and his medical team by his side until the very end, Greg was never hopeless. Social media is filled with beautiful and funny memories of Greg. A dear friend tagged some posts with, "livelikegreg." To live like Greg would be an accomplishment, an honor, even a victory. As I look towards raising Belle and Abe, I look to each of you to cultivate Greg's energy and presence. I will try and remember people's names, to laugh more often, to cultivate patience, and to take time to help others. When swamped with the sadness and mystery of being human, I will think of Greg and the power of hope against all odds. My dearest Greg, go in peace and in love.

Give Sorrow Words

Spirit Self

The other day, a non-medical family member shared the opinion that the medical practice of geriatrics wouldn't be much fun. He noted that elderly people are in decline (he is in his 70s). Although he didn't say this, I imagine he envisioned an impatient doctor sitting twirling a pen while a little old person sits and complains about bowel habits, aches and pains, and other signs of the body's aging.

I begged to differ. My sense is that doctors who choose geriatrics love what they do. Like pregnancy, aging is not a sickness, but a natural part of humanity. The messy confusing parts of life are the ones that reveal ways in which our bodies, minds, and spirits are intertwined. Older people can be calmer, more focused on what is important in life. They've lived through their biggest mistakes, perhaps less likely to repeat them. They have amazing stories, built on experiences that younger people will never, ever share. A time without electronics, a time when milk could be delivered to your front door, a time when women stayed home to care for children and maintain the house.

I've heard that babies and older people are closest to the divine – to that mysterious space at the beginning and end of life when the body is weak but the core of being human, the spirit, is strong and pulsing. I imagine that when a child or an older person dies, their spirit is filled with power. A child spirit may lack wisdom and experience, but it is close to the spark that brought the body into the world. Older people's bodies may be in decline, but their spirit is rich and strong – layers upon layers of loss and laughter, like sedimentary rock.

I wonder about Greg's spirit. He was so physical – athletics, chopping firewood, lifting Belle and Abe into the air. In the last weeks of his life, I felt very little grief –I was buoyed by his physical presence (I'm pretty sure there was some denial going on, too). The help he needed towards the end was around meeting physical needs – eating and drinking, brushing teeth, getting from one place to another, even going to the bathroom. This focus on meeting his physical needs was grounding. When he died, I felt great peace in the presence of his body. I even had a sense of calm holding a box of his dusty, broken ashes.

I sense that his spirit may be confused and even disoriented without the vessel of his strong and powerful body. At the prime of his life, his spirit was furthest from the divinity of birth and from the grace of old age. I've not felt a strong spiritual presence from Greg. There was a day when I was sitting at the computer trying to find the phone number of an acquaintance I hadn't spoken to in months. At the exact time I pulled up her contact information, my phone rang and it was her. She reached out to me at the precise moment I was looking to outreach to her. I believe Greg had something to do with that connect. I think of him constantly. I miss him constantly – sometimes an ache beneath the surface and sometimes a punch in the gut. Greg's and my spirit selves need time to find each-other, to connect in a way that is new for both of us. Some families find their loved ones' spirit in nature – often in the presence of a rainbow. I'll keep my heart open to finding Greg's presence away from the warmth of his skin, the beat of his footsteps, and pure joy of his smile.

Grief Imagined

I hate going through the day without Greg. I hate not hearing his voice. I hate wandering around the grocery story trying to figure out how our meals will work without him. I hate sitting at my work desk, looking across downtown Durham knowing that he won't call and we won't be meeting for lunch. I hate the empty passenger seat next to me. I hate the reminder on my thermostat telling me it's time to change our air filters. Greg carefully kept up with this task. I hate seeing his protein drink sitting on the shelf – the one he would grab and drink down as he was running out the door to bike to an early MRI appointment at the cancer center, leaving the empty container in the sink for me to rinse.

Most of all, I hate bedtime. During his last few weeks at home, unable to walk upstairs, Greg slept in our downstairs guest bed. I slept with him. I couldn't stand the thought of him downstairs alone. I couldn't stand being away from him at night. Our upstairs bedroom became the guest room, with sweet Abe crashing there along with whatever friend or family member was visiting. After Greg died, Belle, Abe, and I all slept together in Greg's and my bed. We developed habits compatible only with summer break. We went to bed late and slept in late, the three of us tumbled into a pile in the middle of our king-sized mattress.

Once school started, I reformed our sloppy sleeping arrangements. The kids had to get to bed in time to get enough sleep before their 6:30a wake up. I needed time in the evenings to make lunches, clean up dishes, and get ready for the next day. We're only a few days in, but the kids transitioned back to their old bedtime routines fairly easily. Per his request, I slept in Abe's bed with him once or twice, joining him after I finished up what I needed to do. For the first few school nights, the kids were in their own beds at a somewhat reasonable time. The weekend switched back to a slumber party in my bed.

My evenings without Greg ache. We used to get to bed as soon as reasonably possible after the kids were down. We had a comfortable flow of evening hygiene, sharing stories from the day, and ogling and laughing at Facebook posts from Greg's wild and wacky circle. Going to bed alone has climbed to near the top of my hate list. The house hums quietly as I putter around finishing chores. I check my phone. I look at the piles of papers I still need to sort through. I ponder my ever-growing to do list. Greg's void drapes heavily over the house. Sometime after eleven, I find my way to the stairs and head up. The emptiness, the feeling of missing him is almost unbearable. I sleep enough to function and wake up to start the day.

I'm able to get through the day OK. With school having started, we're back to familiar rhythms. I'm back at work. I offer genuine smiles to neighbors and coworkers. I tell people about our trip to Montana. I accept words of support and concern, remembrances of the joy Greg carried with him. I share an occasional meal with friends and family. As each day comes to an end, I imagine I feel the way some actors feel. They've interacted with coworkers, talking though ways to make each scene better. They've worked hard, enjoying what they do. As they leave work, heading home down the highway, they've spent most of the day pretending to be somebody they're not. Like these actors, the smiling, working, chatting me doesn't feel like the real me at all.

What would the real me choose instead? If I could, I'd pack a small suitcase, and Belle, Abe, and I would head off to a remote, deserted island. One with abundant food and no stinging or biting creatures. There would be no school, no work, no cell phones, no cars, no dishes, no to-do lists, no mail, no other humans. The three of us would gather fruit in the morning and invent games under a tree near the ocean during the day. We'd write "I love Daddy" in the sand, decorating the words with shells and leaves and moss. When the wind or waves wiped our words away, we'd laugh and pile sand into a sculpture shaped like a bike. We'd build a bonfire in the evenings and as the sun set, I'd tell them my favorite Greg stories. I'd sing them songs from our wedding and tell them about how we took dancing lessons for our first dance. At night, we'd look to the night sky for shooting stars, wishing for things we know won't come true. Once we were tired and bored, once we'd emptied some of our grief into the oceans and the heavens, we'd find our way back home.

Since Greg died, several people have given me books or articles about grief. I read one sent to me by a friend whose wife died from a brain tumor about two years ago. The rest are tucked into the bookshelf next to my bed. I look forward to reading them.

I've thought about how to describe my grief. Growing up, we lived behind a family where the husband was a world-renowned expert in Germanic fairy tales. Their house was decorated with elaborate dioramas of Little Red Riding Hood. For now, my grief feels like one of his fairy tales. This time, instead of a deserted island, my imagination takes me to a thick, dark forest in a northern Eastern Bloc country. There is an Enchantress who owns grief. She looks like a character from Lord of the Rings (if I watched Game of Thrones, then she could come from that set just as well). After night falls, she walks through the forest collecting what she needs for her work. Into her satchel, she gathers shells from unhatched eggs that fell from the nest too soon, and the broken bones of small animals left behind in predator scat. She scrapes away charred bark from lightening that hit a giant tree. She finds bits of fur left behind from a baby rabbit, separated from its mother when it got caught in thorny bramble. She collects dormant seeds lying still beneath the earth, deprived of the right mix of light and moisture needed to grow.

After collecting her items from the forest, she takes them back to her dark, candlelit home and mixes them, crushing the elements with a mortar and pestle, forming them into small orbs of sadness and lost moments. Before dawn, she travels the earth in search of people who have gone through a recent loss. As they lay sleeping, she slips an orb into them, guiding it through their sternum, deep inside. And there it sits. Nobody can see it, but the person suffering feels a new weight of sadness. Some people only feel the dark, heavy weight of grief in their core. For others, the orb rests inside in ways that disrupt their heart, their pulse, their digestion. Once placed, the Enchantress has done her job. She plays no part in determining how each person will continue to live with the dark sphere she has placed. She goes onto the next home, taking her magic and leaving the person alone to learn how to live with this new feeling.

Back in the real world, there is no island to escape to, no Enchantress. Our severed three pack will be out and about, at work, at school, at church, at the grocery store. We will cry. We will smile. We will sleep alone and then tumble back in bed together when we need to. We will learn how to manage our grief, just as people have done for ages before us and will continue to do once our time is done. We will find ways to remember Greg, to carry him with us. Over time, we will form a new Greg, one of memories and of acts of kindness and laughter, brought forth all that he boldly shared during our time together.

Fierce

I've been struggling with writing, thinking of taking a break. Thoughts and emotions ebb and flow, but my ability to translate them into words feels daunting. I am continually overwhelmed with the mechanics of getting through the day. My aching grief is intense. My dedication to and love for Belle and Abe are intense. Work is intense. The piles and piles and piles of paperwork are intense. It is rare for me to get a sliver of actual time to process and write.

The title "Fierce" comes from my emotions around Belle and Abe. I am driven by the need to shepherd them through the mechanics and emotions of losing their beautiful, amazing, strong father. By the need to get through 24 hours physically and mentally intact. Nothing about my grief changed. Nothing. We ache, all the time.

Paperwork has become my albatross. There are piles everywhere.

I take baby-steps to tackle important things like bills for electricity and water, but the flood of documentation pours into my mailbox every day. I need to refinance our mortgage. Abe has first communion this year. Greg has stacks of medical bills. I need to capture Greg's dedication to retirement by managing his retirement accounts. We have home and auto insurance. I need to pay Belle and Abe's tuition. Christmas is coming. Social Security needs proof that I'm not blowing Belle and Abe's money on frivolous purchases. The neighborhood association gives violations for firewood stacks in the side yard. Abe is starting basketball this year. Paperwork is everywhere, all the time.

When I think of Belle and Abe, I feel fierce. When I think of Greg, I feel love and passion and emptiness and questions and answers and a long, long road ahead. When I think of me, I feel gratitude for the circle of support I have and I feel achy and empty for the chasm Greg left behind.

Sixty-five More Years

When Greg and I got married, he proclaimed, "Here's to 65 more years." This became one of our go-to, lovey-dovey musings. Even after 12 years of marriage, I couldn't bring myself to ever subtract a year from our marital forecast – I decided that we would just have to work on our prolonging our lifespan. Far into Greg's cancer diagnosis, we would still reference our unfolding 65 years together. We were never cocksure about him being cured, but we also held onto the belief that he would live a very long time.

I remember appointments at the cancer center where his doctor assured us that they could treat his cancer and that he would live to see Belle and Abe's milestones of graduations and weddings. His doctor would come into our room and say, "I just saw a patient with your same tumor type. She was diagnosed 23 years ago and is doing great." We were hopeful. As the saying goes, "At Duke, There is Hope."

Stumbling through the grief process, most often pushing it aside, I realize that I am still reeling from Greg's rapid decline and death. Even after two surgeries and one biopsy in 6-months, I really thought that his oncology team would ultimately get his cancer under control long enough for us to settle into some sense of remission. On May 14, 2016, Greg won first place in a state BMX race in Charlotte. This was the 10th race he needed to move from Novice class into Intermediate class.

On May 23rd, 2016 he had a stable scan. On July 14th, 2016, Greg passed away.

The five weeks between our ED visit on June 9th and his death crushed me in a way that I am still trying to understand. I have gotten to know two other widows who each have two school-aged children and whose husbands died from cancer in the past year. We have talked about the trauma of those last few weeks of our husbands' lives. "Trauma" can be an overused word, but the intensity of watching a once vibrant man in his 40s move into complete loss of function and eventually life is crushing.

Greg tried so desperately to make the best of every situation and this is the tone we set in the weeks before he died. During those weeks, he shit in his pants and lost the ability to pee, his legs weakened and he eventually lost the ability to walk, he needed help organizing his medications and getting a drink of water, he fell down, he slept for extended periods of time, he became confused, he had seizures, and eventually, he stopped eating and drinking.

In the four years of living with cancer, he only asked for pain medicine one time. Once during that last trip to RI, he asked for Tylenol for a headache. That's the only complaint of pain I ever heard from him. Those who were part of the inner circle those past few weeks will probably smile in remembering his constant desire for backscratching. He wanted, he needed, to have his back scratched 24-7. His parents, friends, and I would work in shifts, sitting at the side of his bed, scratching, scratching, scratching until our shoulders ached. He wasn't picky about the style of scratching – gentle or firm, circles or sweeps – he just needed his back scratched. My last nights next to him were filled with back scratching and catheterizing him. He was never shy or self-conscious about either need. Now, when I tuck Belle and Abe into bed and scratch their backs, I remember their Dad and the calm this brought him as he barreled towards death.

Right now, I am still caught in the surprise and ache of these last few weeks. I find myself remembering his inherent strength and humor and the dramatic way cancer sucked everything away so quickly. I know that for many, death comes even more unexpectedly. Even, so, I wasn't ready for the end. Our sixty-five years were never guaranteed, but I sure did want them.

Single

Being a single, working, grieving parent is grueling. I wake around 5a, get to bed around 10p, and am running non-stop the whole time. I have a terrible time getting the kids to bed on time – dinner, homework, practicing music, giving them a little time to unwind, and going through the bedtime routine seems to take forever. I am struck by the weight of being responsible for everything – for every aspect of working, of parenting, and of trying to keep the house in order. Dishes, firewood, going through mail, planning and preparing meals, planning birthdays, making sure the kids have enough underwear, paying bills and keeping up with account balances, and on and on and on.

I am still immersed in paperwork. I am actively working with an estate attorney, a financial planner, and an accountant for taxes. Each of these pieces are important to our family's security, are very time consuming, and really can only be done by me. I'm hoping the bulk of this paperwork will be done by April. Then, there is still more paperwork (Greg has boxes of it), but the big stuff will hopefully be done.

I miss Greg terribly, but have a hard time expressing my sadness. I feel his presence all the time – not so much like a ghost or a spirit, but his energy, his voice, his wisdom, his joy. I still do not understand his not being here, his not coming back. The mental energy of getting through the day pushes my sadness down into a still and quiet place within.

What Ifs?

It is hard to not look back and wonder if we could have done things differently to change the outcome of Greg's disease. There are brain tumor patients who talk and write about knowing that they will beat their disease. Every public expression is one of confidence and determination regarding their ability to survive their diagnosis. Greg and I never had complete confidence that his cancer would go into remission. We navigated the wash of doubt and fear that came with each scan and were magnified with each recurrence. Through these doubts, we always wanted the cancer to go away, to give him a break, to step back into the shadows so that he could focus on other things.

I've worried that our doubts and fears were some barrier to his ability to beat his cancer. The confidence I see in other patients feels like magical thinking to me, but maybe this magic is what is really behind the body's ability to kill the cancer cells. People love miracles, love survivors, love beating the odds. The news is full of stories of those people who beat the odds, whose metastatic stage 4 cancer melts away. So often the patients in these stories say, "I always knew I would win." The stories of loss, of succumbing to disease, are harder to find – tucked away in obituaries and personal blogs.

I am scientifically minded, a concrete thinker. As true as I try to be to my emotions, the magical thinking theory of beating cancer doesn't feel right to me. I have a hard time accepting that deep knowledge of a cure against all other odds is somehow the magical elixir to halting cancer cells. Years ago, perhaps decades, I read a book on dreams called, "*Where People Fly and Water Runs Uphill*" (Jeremy Taylor, Grand Central Publishing, 1992).The author tells the story of a woman who went to the doctor for abdominal pain and the doctors couldn't find anything wrong. The woman kept having dreams that she had rotting meat in her purse. I don't remember the details, but in the end, she was diagnosed with some type of abdominal or reproductive cancer. Her dreams of the rotting meat were her body's way of letting her know that something was wrong inside.

Cancer cells divide and divide inside the body, changing their genetic make-up, creating and responding to proteins. I wonder if those cells and proteins somehow communicate with the healthy, functioning part of our brains and bodies. Perhaps the interplay between our healthy cells and the proteins and cells of cancer are what lead people to either knowing that they can beat the cancer or to having fears and doubts about the cancer's strength. Greg's cancer exploded through his nervous system in a way that shocked his doctors. Somewhere buried in the genetic code of his particular tumor was something that said "go" – do not respond to chemo, do not respond to radiation – just go, go, go. Rather than fretting that we failed to cultivate a sense of optimism that never took hold, I take a bit of comfort in thinking that maybe Greg's cancer gave him reason to worry, that the sneaky, devilish proteins of his tumor cells screamed danger all along.

Outside of our emotional journey, I also wonder if there are "what ifs" to his treatment or to how he lived his life after diagnosis. We always deferred to his oncologist's recommendations for treatment. What if we stopped after one surgery? I remember noticing after his second surgery how the hole where the cancer was now connected as an opening to one of his ventricles. I remember wondering what cancer cells would do in this situation. His oncologist liked to start treatment with a clean slate in terms of tumors. His neurosurgeon always said that the re-growth was small, but that he would defer to the oncology team regarding treatment. Because Greg's tumor was easily accessible (from a surgical perspective), because he generally did well after surgery, because Duke has the best neurosurgeon in the world, the direction was always towards more surgery. In hindsight, I wonder if we should have held off. Greg has a friend with the same tumor type that is inoperable. He is alive, in treatment, and doing relatively well. So far, chemo and radiation have kept his tumor from growing.

I don't fault his cancer team in their decisions. I am sure that the vast majority of the time, treatment does go better with a clean slate. The incidence of Greg's tumor type metastasizing is exceedingly rare. There are only a handful of cases reported in all the literature. Still, part of me expects that at some point down the road, there will be a genetic test that reveals a rare mutation that leads to the explosion of cancer cells that happened with Greg.

I have other layers of "what-ifs" around our day-to-day life after Greg was diagnosed. Greg always ate well and exercised. Some cancer patients go to extremes with their diet – there are numerous cancer diets out there, most involving eliminating sugar and carbs. Others go to great lengths to shift the body towards a more alkaline state than an acidic state. These diets are hard to follow and haven't been scientifically proven. Even so, there are people who report anecdotal success these dramatic shifts in their body's fuel. Greg never made drastic changes to his diet. On occasion, he would order a Pepsi with his black bean burrito. He would have a beer at the end of a long day. I sometimes wonder if his cancer could have been tamed with one of the more extreme diets – if, in addition to his treatment at the cancer center, cutting off sugar would have tilted things in his favor.

I will never know the answers to my "what ifs". If I knew we could make a change and go back in time to change it, then I would jump at the chance. What I do know, is that up until his last breath, Greg was always true to himself and to the people around him. He lived the life he wanted to live in virtually every way he could. As a husband, as a father, as an engineer, as an athlete, as a friend, as a volunteer, he followed his spirit and instincts for kindness and generosity and hard work and love.

He always, always brought laughter with him wherever he went. As I look back over an ocean of maybes and what-ifs, I never once question Greg's spirit. Everybody who remembers him, remembers his authentic self. We hold him in love and as a guide to us to live our lives with the greatness that burst forth from him every single day.

Searching

Your grieving is among the most sacred and the most human things
you will ever do.
It will unfold to you the mystery of life...
and death...
and rebirth.
Honor it.

Sometime during the past year, I came across this quote. After months went by, I couldn't remember where I read the quote, but I knew I liked it. I searched around, asked around, and learned that it came from Duke Bereavement services. I felt like something had gone full circle. The same institution that tried to convince me that, "At Duke, There is Hope" was now telling me that my grief is sacred. Life is messy.

If nothing else, over the past year, I've felt grief as a spiritual journey. The death of my soul mate left me raw, confused, overwhelmed, and open to a presence I'd not seriously considered before. Every night, I tell Greg that I love him and that I miss him. I speak the words aloud, gently breathing my energy into the space around me, sensing that the hum of my words may connect to him in some way.

Two nights ago, I put in an Indigo Girls CD, a tried and true from college. The lyrics from one of my favorite songs say, "If we wait for the time 'til all souls get it right, then at least I know there'll be no nuclear annihilation in my lifetime. I'm still not right" (Rites of Passage, 1992). True that, I thought. I'm definitely still not right.

Your grieving is among the most sacred and the most human things you will ever do.

Since having children, I've felt like I should do something to recognize the summer (and winter) solstice. When Belle and Abe were at preschool, the lead teacher offered concrete opportunities to recognize the rhythm of the seasons. She created the spiritual space of spiral walks and lantern walks and candle making and May crownings. Without The Children's Garden, I feel untethered to our planet's journey through space – to the blessings of spring, summer, fall, winter. This most recent summer solstice I felt grumpy, resigned to my inability to carve out time and space to connect to a journey greater and more magical than the one consumed by work and chores and daily survival.

At the end of the day on this year's summer solstice, I thought of Duke's bereavement quote, I thought of my day, and I realized that what felt pedantic and lacking in meaning was actually filled with blessings. No, I didn't create a deliberate space or ceremony to acknowledge the day with the greatest number of hours of sunlight. I did have coffee with a woman Greg met a year or so earlier. He met her at the cancer center café, after she made an unsolicited wise crack to him about riding his bike to his appointments. At that time, she'd just been diagnosed with breast cancer and was awaiting her treatment plan. She was Canadian, and Greg charmed her with his recognition of Canadian accents and a Terry Fox coin he always kept in his backpack. This connection helped them with the burdens of treatment. The same day after coffee with Greg's Canadian connection, I got a text from a brain tumor patient who learned that the tumor had started to grow again and surgery would be in the next few days. This person was one of the first patients Greg learned about after his diagnosis who turned to running and exercise as part of the healing journey. I immediately texted back – "When can we meet?" All day, I wanted to cry, feeling the weight of this news. I also spent time on life and disability insurance paperwork – good times. For all of my self-imposed "shoulds" on this day of maximum sunlight, I did what I needed to do. I made the most of what I had. I had moments that filled my soul, bared my heart, and connected me to Greg.

It will unfold to you the mystery of life...

Scrolling through posts and comments on Facebook, I am both struck and guiltily annoyed by declarations of God's hand among cancer survivors. Just a few words I've come across:

HE is in charge!
Prayers will continue as you recover. God bless you.
God's Blessings!
Amazing! God is good!

I'm pretty sure I have a bias, but I've always had a strong sense that blessings and declarations of God's presence are strong during a survivors' fight and then dwindle dramatically if somebody dies. Somewhat ironically, I also believe that God is most present, most tangible, in the space surrounding birth and death. God was with us at the hospice home, as I lay next to Greg's slowing body. Back to my brain tumor connect who recently needed surgery for another recurrence – one of the Facebook posts went something along the lines of:

What kind of tumor do you have?
The only tumor with God in the name!!
Oligodendroglioma?
Yes!

This is the same tumor type as Greg. I immediately felt anger well in my belly. Seriously? We're finding God in the fricking name of the tumor type? Is God not present for folks with other tumor types? Is God still present when this same tumor explodes through your entire nervous system causing all functions to cease? I care about this friend who is fighting cancer and didn't feel I had good reason for my anger. Later, I realized that this survivor, this friend of Greg's, is scared, deeply scared. My guess, my gut, is that for this person, finding God in every single nook and cranny brings some calm to the storm, releases the fist of fear clinched tightly around any sense of normalcy. For this person, God is in running and God is in surviving prior surgeries and God is in the doctors' hands and by golly, God is in the name of the tumor type. I had no reason to be upset.

Looking through Greg's Facebook page, I see this comment: "Greg, keep on biking in heaven." The threads of faith continue for some, even when our loved one is gone.

and death...
and rebirth.
Honor it.

Over the past week, I've realized that I am struggling with acts that represent letting go. I still wear my wedding ring. Greg's closet is still filled with his clothes and boxes of baseball and hockey cards. People ask me what I'm doing on July 14th, the year anniversary of Greg's death. Honestly, I don't want to do a darn thing. There is nothing about this day that makes me want to do anything other than maybe stay in bed with the lights out. The thought of taking off my wedding ring, of cleaning Greg's closet, of recognizing the day he died – it all feels like a punch in the gut. I am depressed by the prospect of starting another year without him.

Still, whatever I feel, whatever I want, my life continues without Greg. I need to continue loving Belle and Abe. I need to keep working. I need to recognize the moments of love and grace that my circle shines upon me. After dropping Belle and Abe off after dinner, my parents say, "We have an idea for what to do on Friday to remember Greg. We should go see the new Spider Man movie. That's something he would do, something he would like. We can go to the columbarium and then go to the movies." They are right – Greg and I always loved superhero movies.

So, there you have it. A year that began with my husband's last breath looks to be ending with a family gathering and a Spiderman movie. Lots happened in-between. More than ever before, I have a feeling of love and energy beyond what my five senses can take in. I feel Greg's presence around me and I know that my spirit still has work to do.

Epilogue

After Greg died, I knew that there was no way I could keep up with all of his firewood work. I figured I would go back to Craigslist – spend more money, burn less wood, and do my best to savor the memories from past winters. Instead, Drew stepped in to fill Greg's steel toed boots. A few months after Greg died, he brought trailers of wood to our house and organized friends to help with splitting and stacking. Through Drew's organizing and efforts, nine people came together to split and process enough wood to refill our racks. Young and old, they worked to keep up the tradition that brought so much fulfillment to Greg and allowed him to give both literal and emotional warmth to his family. There was still a small amount of wood left that Greg split – who knew that firewood could be sentimental, a spiritual connection to the deceased?

Months went by where I opened our tool shed for a hammer or to pull out one of the kid's bikes and walked past Greg's chopping equipment. I glanced down at the wood handle and heavy metal head and stepped past it for whatever item I was looking for. After a winter of burning the wood gathered from friends, I outreached to Drew to ask if he would show me how to use Greg's maul to split wood. We met in his back yard and he showed me how to stand, how to hold the tool, and how to swing. I was nervous, clumsy, and self-conscious. After about 30 minutes, I split two smaller pieces. I gathered my items, offered a hug of gratitude to him and his wife, and headed home.

Back home, I decided to try my hand at splitting alone. My first try took about 45 minutes to split one round in half (it's possible it was gum, or something of the sort.). I kept at it for several days. Just a week or so later, I could split and stack a full cart in that time. I learned the nuanced sounds when the maul hits the wood – a deep thud or a higher pitched crack. I look at the top of a round and see where to aim the first strike, perhaps hitting a fissure on my first or second try. The physical demands, the sweat gathering on my back, the sounds, and the earthy, aromatic smell of wood are all so satisfying.

Sometimes, there is a spark when the metal first hits the wood. The flash is tiny, appearing and disappearing so quickly, like the first firefly of summer. I've swung the maul hundreds of times by now, seen a spark maybe ten times. I am surprised every time. As I put away the tools and gloves, cover the wood with a rain tarp, I wonder if I am wasting my time spending hours and hours chopping firewood while standing next to the fan unit of my HVAC. Later, shoulders aching, laundry piled with dirt and sweat and saw-dust covered clothes, I feel like chopping firewood is the only solitary part of my day, my week, with any real meaning.

I wish, with a deep, profound ache, that the beautiful Gränsfors Bruks mauls were still in Greg's hands. I wish I could share my joy and satisfaction with him. In his absence, I am filled with gratitude that I have worked to tackle this skill on my own. I can hear Greg saying, "I knew you could do it."

Made in the USA
Columbia, SC
17 September 2020

20811570R00119